DRESS BETTER FOR LESS

by Vicki Audette

Meadowbrook Press

18318 Minnetonka Boulevard
Deephaven, Minnesota 55391

To my sons, Jim and Dave Audette,
who lived this experience with me.

First printing August, 1981

The quote from Egon Von Fürstenberg on pg. 27 is from
The Power Look by Egon Von Fürstenberg, published by
Holt, Rinehart and Winston. Copyright © 1978 by Egon
Von Fürstenberg. Reprinted with permission.

The quotes from Venita Van Caspel on pg. 18 are from pgs.
54 and 55 of *Money Dynamics for the 1980's* by Venita Van
Caspel. Reprinted with permission of Reston Publishing
Co., a Prentice-Hall Co., 11480 Sunset Hills Road, Reston,
VA 22090.

Printed in the United States of America
ISBN (paperback): 0–915658–33–X
ISBN (hardcover): 0–915658–44–5

Library of Congress Cataloging in Publication Data

Audette, Vicki.
  Dress better for less.

  Includes index.
  1. Clothing and dress. I. Title.
TX340.A93   646'.3   81–11246
ISBN 0–915658–44–5   AACR2
ISBN 0–915658–33–X (pbk.)

Cover Designer and Art Director: Terry Dugan
Text Designer: Sandra Falls
Production Manager: John Ware
Illustrators: Judith Meyeraan, Michele Zylman
Photographer: G. Robert Spencer
Managing Editor: Kathe Grooms
Editor: Amy Rood

Contents

Acknowledgments

A special thank you to a talented bargain hunter, friend and long-time shopping partner Arlene Faricy; to all the wonderful people at Steeple People Thrift Store for their support; to my associate researchers Martha Fisk, Patty Navin, Sonja Olsen and my initial researcher Mary Anne Kowalski; to my sewing consultant Neil Hede; to my vintage clothing and jewelry consultant Lois Rovick; to household-hints expert Lois Millner for sharing her unique, tried-and-true stain removal methods; to Jack McGuire and the staff at Anthonie's for their tips on quality classic clothing; to my father Roy Sturdivant who shared his experience and interest; to my sister Nancy Toler for her total encouragement; to Michael Olmstead for his invaluable help; and to all my family, friends and business associates who offered their suggestions, humor and guidance during the writing of this book, especially Al Janicke, Beth Sosin, Ray Conover, Mary Singher, Joy Sturdivant, Bev Krautkremer, Steve Edelman, Sharon Anderson and Kim Sturdivant. Many thanks are owed to my publishers Bruce and Vicki Lansky for shaping the direction of this book, and to my editor Kathe Grooms for her professional assistance in making this endeavor possible.

Introduction

No matter what your budget or taste is in clothes, it's certain that you want the best possible quality at the best price. Too many people assume that you have to sacrifice one or the other—quality or savings. But bargain hunters know you can get both. You just need to know their secrets!

If you don't know those secrets, you may find it hard to believe that you *can* get the best for very little. This book is designed to tell you those secrets. With it you will

- **Learn to recognize** high performance, top quality clothing.

- **Avoid paying** full price for it.

- **Get all the mileage** you can from the clothes you buy.

Regardless of what kind of clothes you shop for—new, discount or second-hand—you'll learn to dress better for less.

Once you get the knack, you'll discover the thrill of bargain shopping and making your own finds. Whether you're an office worker following John Molloy's formulas for "dressing for success," a preppy, a parent keeping your growing kids' wrists and ankles covered, or a homemaker who is after fashionable casual clothes that won't warp your budget, the tips, techniques and sources of clothes in this book will put fun back into your shopping and keep money in your pockets.

Times have changed in the clothing industry. The 1980's will be known as the "discount decade." In response to increasing demands for better clothes that don't cost so much, retailers have begun marking prices down earlier in each clothing season and reincarnating bargain basements in their retail stores. Discount and factory outlet stores are cropping up in every city, while second-hand sources are giving them a literal run for their money. Resale shops, church thrift stores, Salvation Army and Goodwill stores, rummage sales and garage sales are enticing shoppers who never before bought second-hand clothes to take advantage of the unbelievable bargains they offer. If you aren't helping yourself to these bargains yet, you're in for a wonderful surprise: the best clothing doesn't have to cost a lot!

I'd like to be your shopping guide and introduce you to every imaginable way you can save money on better clothes. If you haven't shopped some of these sources before, particularly the second-hand ones, you may be skeptical about prices. I outfitted the models on the cover of this book with clothing I bought mostly at second-hand sources. His business suit would have cost $357.00 new. I paid only $68.50 for it. Her outfit would have cost $253.00 new. I paid only $39.00. You might think it takes an admitted bargain shark like me to find these bargains. But trust me: in this book I've condensed more than 20 years of experience to give you all the information you need.

Use the wardrobe worksheets, the tips on shopping specific types of clothing sources, the fashion and consumer resource lists, the directories of bargain clothes sellers and the wealth of information in this book, and I guarantee that you'll see a big difference in the money you need to spend on clothes. And what's more, you'll be getting better quality and wear for your dollars—or cents. So happy bargain hunting!

Vicki Audette

Finding Gold in Your Closet

The starting point on the way to dressing better for less is to appraise your present wardrobe honestly and creatively. If your closet is full of wearable clothes you just don't wear, you're wasting precious space and money. Evaluate each item objectively, and then keep the items you can wear "as is." Turn the deadbeat clothes—your true duds—into cold cash and use some of the money to alter and transform last year's fashions into today's look.

Don't let a good wool suit bite the dust before you've considered your updating options (see pages 122–125), unless you're just fed up with it! An alteration or makeover may help you avoid expensive clothing replacement costs.

How to Appraise Your Closet

Your closet survey will save you unnecessary shopping time and money as well. Take a look at the chart on page 8, and consider your profit-making options. Here's an example of what you might find in your own appraisal.

Raising fashion consciousness

• **Study up.** Women: flip thru *Vogue*, *Glamour*, *Cosmopolitan*, *Harper's Bazaar*, *Mademoiselle*, *Big Beautiful Woman*, *Seventeen*, *Working Woman*, *Essence*. Men: try *Gentleman's Quarterly*, *Esquire*, *Playboy*. Look also at pattern catalogs in fabric shops for ideas for both men and women. Children: the catalogs are great: Sears, Penney's, Ward's.

• **Steal ideas.** Look at the ad layouts. Look for the current combinations of color and fabric. Pay special attention to styling details: hemlines, widths of collars and lapels, other trends. Notice what types of accessories are used and how they're worn (see pages 149–151).

• **Recombine garments.** Apply your fashion-keen eye to your own outfits, seeing them as raw material for new combinations.

Appraising a wardrobe

I usually start a wardrobe appraisal by inviting a friend to join me. It's more fun, and two heads are better than one. Make sure you've got a well-lit, full-length mirror and some pins so you can try out instant alteration ideas.

• **Take** everything out of your closet and drawers. Put aside out-of-season things so you can focus on the present.

Solid blazer with plaid skirt

Solid blazer with solid skirt

- **Separate** your clothes into three categories. "Wearables" are clothes you will keep and wear without any changes. "Alterables" are clothes worth keeping if they are worth altering (see page 130). "Sellables" are clothes you can find no use for, altered or otherwise. Plan to resell, donate or even trade them (see page 6).

Mixing and matching wearables

The object here is to get at least five outfits out of the two you already have. It can be done. Use your knowledge of current fashion and a little imagination, and suddenly your outfits will take on a new value as you capitalize on their versatility.

- **Toss** a pair of tweed slacks next to a striped blazer or shirt. You may be pleased with the effect.

- **Belt** a cardigan sweater, or tuck it into a skirt.

- **Break up** suits and three-piece outfits and wear their parts as separates. There's no law that says you can't wear your navy sportcoat with your tan suit pants.

- **Combine** a dress with a blazer to give it a "working look."

Giving new life to alterables

You'll be amazed at how much more fashion mileage you can get from old and worn clothing if you consider the possibility of somehow altering it.

- **Update** outfits by narrowing a pair of wide-leg slacks or by getting a collar or cuff changed to reflect current "standards."

- **Visualize** saving only part of a garment: a dress becoming a tunic top, a pair of pants becoming shorts (see page 131).

- **Repair** (or have repaired) any frayed edges, holes and so on, by turning collars, applying patches, changing lengths of hems or sleeves, and so on.

Discovering personal buying habits

A few years ago I helped a friend do a closet appraisal. It was astonishing to see how much we learned about her personal buying habits. Since then, whenever I appraise my own wardrobe I ask myself the following questions to keep from making past buying mistakes again and to make the most of past successes.

- **Do I have a surplus of a single cut, color, fabric or pattern?** I want to avoid them when shopping.

- **Do I have an outfit I am dissatisfied with?** Maybe it wrinkled too easily or just didn't hold up in the wearing. I want to make note of the fabric, the manufacturer, the cut—and not buy a similar item again. Just the opposite goes for the favorites.

- **Did I buy an outfit that was trendy at the time, but later could not be updated?** This can be a real buying mistake if the item is costly.

For example, one year I bought a Calvin Klein suit. Later the blazer could not be shortened, because the detail on the back was too involved and altering it would have distorted the balance of the jacket. Next time I bought a more simple style (see page 42).

Recognizing sellables

If you don't know what to do with the clothes in your "sellable" pile, or you haven't put any clothes into it, the following tips may help you recognize and turn a profit on the "deadwood" in your wardrobe. Remember, what won't fit your clothing needs may fit someone else's. Earn some money by not keeping an item for the following reasons.

• **Diet plans:** if you are holding onto it because you think you'll lose weight someday, but you have 25 pounds to go.

• **Bad colors:** if you have a stylish dress or suit, but the color has never been right for you, no matter what state your tan was in.

• **Guilt:** if you paid too much for an outfit that you don't wear often. Are you only keeping it out of guilt? Why not earn some of its cost back and reinvest in a more useable item?

Cleaning your closet out

To turn those sellables into cold cash, choose one or more of the following methods. You'll relish the extra space in your closet and the extra money in your pocket. For more tips on how to do these things, see chapters 2 and 5.

• **Throw a sale.** Hold a garage, yard or apartment sale, either by yourself or with others. You won't pocket a bundle, but your sellables will be gone—and it's fun.

• **Rent space** at a flea market if you find you have a real load to get rid of. The crowds coming by will be much larger than those you'll entice to a private sale, so your odds of selling everything are better. But there are two drawbacks: the rental fee (approximately $25.00) and the trouble of hauling goods to the site.

• **Resell.** If you're not a vendor at heart, get somebody else to do it for you—take your clothes to a resale shop (also called a consignment shop). You'll have to split your take with the shop, but the clothes will be out of your hands and the money in your pocket. However, only fashionable, clean clothes in good condition will interest resellers.

• **Donate.** This last alternative won't line your pockets with gold, but it can lessen your tax bite. Donate your sellables to charitable groups, who run thrift stores or rummage sales. Ask a drycleaner (see page 21) to determine the value of your donations, and be sure to keep your receipt. You may even find a charity willing to pick up your clothes!

Wardrobe Planning Worksheet

Now that you have finished your wardrobe appraisal and weeded out your sellables, make out a shopping list to build on what you're keeping. Note what items these new ones are supposed to go with, too. Just as impulsive grocery shopping can be avoided by carrying a list, so can impulsive clothes shopping. Keep this guide handy in your purse or attaché case.

WHAT I NEED TO ADD TO MY WARDROBE

Basics:

Suits _____

Slacks _____

Shirts _____

Dresses _____

Outerwear:

Coats _____

Jackets _____

Hats _____

Shoes and Accessories:

Shoes _____

Boots _____

Belts _____

Purses _____

Gloves _____

Jewelry _____

Ties _____

Items to Bring Along Shopping
(for color and style match): _____
_____

WHAT I WOULD LOVE TO ADD
(IF BOUGHT CHEAP)

Let yourself go here. You will be pleasantly surprised when you find the item at a garage sale or on a clearance rack.

Trendy Accessories: _____

Special Occasion Outfits: _____

Fantasy Items (furs, jewelry): _____

How to Find Gold in Your Closet

1. Evaluation: Try on everything in your closet and dresser, in front of your spouse, friend or lover—you'll need a second opinion.

2. Performance: Throw—literally—your tweed jacket next to your gabardine slacks. Do they go well together? You should get at least three outfits (five would be great) based on each individual item. If you don't, it's not performing for you.

3. Fit and Style: Examine the clothing that is not performing. Is the fit bad? Can it be altered? If it's too tight, it's not likely that it can be enlarged. If it's not likely that *you* can be reduced, set it in your resale pile. If the lines of lapels, cuffs, collars and so on can be slimmed to match current fashions, consider altering them *if* the fabric and construction make them worth remodeling and *if*, once remodeled, the garment performs well with the rest of your wardrobe.

4. Income: Take everything you've decided not to keep to a resale shop for men, women or children. Let the clerk evaluate what's resellable (that's his specialty). If he'll take some-

thing only if you dryclean it first, ask how he'll price it, what you'll get (you should get 50%), and how much he'd expect a cleaner to charge. Then you can judge your profit margin and act accordingly.

5. Tax Breaks: Donate the leftover clothing to your favorite charity, but don't forget to write it off. Use the information on Fair Market Values (page 21), to appraise your clothes and find their write-off value. (Nobody's ever been questioned on these values!) Be sure the charity gives you an itemized receipt; file it with your tax records.

6. Bottom Line: Suppose you've got three suits, two sportcoats, two pairs of slacks and assorted shirts, ties and sweaters to evaluate. You find:

Suit A   is wearable—no cost, no profit

Suit B   is alterable—net cost $20.00

Suit C   is sellable—net profit $40.00

Donations (tax write-off)—net profit $80.00

Total profit—$100.00—plus a total of 20 new outfits, by mixing the suits, jackets and pants in all possible combinations!

Planning Strategies

Some people can think of nothing they enjoy more than shopping for clothes. For others, the thought of clothes shopping is practically hell on earth! Yet regardless of their feelings about getting clothes, all shoppers seem to agree on one thing: they don't want to waste time *or* money. The key to avoiding those traps is obvious—be sure you're a well-educated shopper, aware of the value of investing in quality clothes.

Ten years ago I tagged along with a friend, Jim, who was shopping for a working wardrobe. We learned a lot that day about what it means to buy quality clothes and to profit from investment dressing.

Jim had just opened a large men's hairstyling salon and needed to look well-groomed and stylishly professional. He preferred not to wear suits to work because of the physical nature of his job. His clothing budget was $250.00.

Fortunately, Jim was helped by a very knowledgeable clothing salesman who steered him to high-yield separates. Jim bought three pairs of all-season, gabardine, imported slacks for $60.00 each and two 100% wool sweaters (to match all three slacks) for $55.00 each. The clothes were beautifully constructed and designed in a simple, ageless style.

At first Jim was hesitant to spend over his budget, as he had never paid that much for one pair of slacks or a sweater before. As it turned out, he never regretted the purchases. Over the years, Jim kept in touch with the salesman and added pieces of the same imported brand (but at sale mark-down prices). The sweaters and slacks he bought ten years ago continue to perform for him: as Jim puts it, "They still grab a compliment." Jim's story shows that to get the most for your money, you must select clothes with lasting value. You can do this at retail store sales, discount stores and all second-hand sources. Whenever you pay less for the best, your clothing dollar is wisely spent.

Design Your Shopping Plan

Plan your wardrobe purchases around your present wardrobe (see page 7). This will help you to budget your expenses and to shop the seasonal sales. It's a good idea to know what percentage of your clothing dollar you will spend on each wardrobe purchase. Then you will get the maximum value out of the clothes you wear the most.

Your clothing dollar

How much you spend on clothes is really determined by your other living expenses and your clothing lifestyle. It's one of the expenses you can cut back on whenever your budget is tight—

by using a careful shopping plan to make the most of your clothing dollar.

Budget a Working Wardrobe

We've all become conscious of the need to dress well for work in offices, thanks to John Molloy's *Dress for Success.* Here are some new wrinkles (the pun intended) on how to arrange a successful office wardrobe on a budget.

Nine-to-five basics for women

In a recent article in *Working Woman* magazine, Judy Hadlock suggested these nine basic wardrobe pieces for women who work in offices: two skirts, two blouses, two blazers, one dress,

12 Smart Shopping Angles

1. Every time you make a purchase, consider the value per wear. If you spend $100.00 on an item that you only wear twice, your value per wear is $50.00 each time you wear it. If you keep this in mind it will make it difficult to justify buying an outfit on purely emotional grounds, unless it is really useful to your wardrobe.

2. Buy quality items, but buy them on sale (most retail merchandise is marked up 100%). Quality items will last longer and give you more value per wear.

3. Spend your clothing dollars on versatile separates that will make several outfits.

4. Shop with a list to avoid impulse buying.

5. Search out bargain sources: bargain basements, discount stores, second-hand places (see page 159).

6. Buy quality clothing for children (see page 136) when it's going to be passed on to other siblings.

7. Figure your clothing allowance and stick to it. Keep tight control of credit buying (see pages 18–19).

8. Be sensible and phone ahead to compare prices and save time.

9. Be aggressive and bargain on top-priced items (see pages 25–26).

10. Read care labels (see page 51). Ask the salesperson about the durability and care of a garment. If the label reads "Dryclean Only," consider the cost of cleaning along with the value per wear.

11. Purchase clothes you know you really like. If you need it, but don't love it, the garment will sit in your closet and in the end it will be an expensive buying mistake.

12. Keep your receipts in order to save time later if you need to return an item. But don't be discouraged if you have lost a receipt. Use your cancelled check, or if you used a credit card, your billing statement. Major department stores keep some record of their sales, so if you have no proof at all, phone ahead and ask them to look through their sales records.

one pair of slacks and one sweater. *Working Wardrobe,* a book by Janet Wallach, also offers suggestions for affordable, versatile working clothes. The section on color is particularly interesting.

• **Mix and match.** Build your basic wardrobe around two or more matchable colors. This will give you a high performance mix and you can wear all of these clothes as interchangeable pieces. For example, match the two blouses and one sweater with all the separates. Both blazers should mix with the dress and the two skirts.

• **Choose two blazers,** one in a solid dark color, the other in a solid medium color.

• **Coordinate your skirts and blouses** by choosing one solid color and one pattern. Make sure one skirt is the same color as one of the blazers. This will give you a suit look when it's necessary.

• **Pick a year-round fabric** for these major wardrobe investments. Gabardine works well for suits, blazers, skirts and slacks. (Invest less in outfits that will be limited to a single season—summer or winter—unless you live in a climate where that season is very long.)

• **Buy shoes in a neutral color** that will work in all seasons. Choose one pair for work, one for dress and one for play.

• **Plan your accessories** to fit your nine-to-five schedule. Choose less jewelry and make it classic enough to fit your evening needs.

Nine-to-five basics for women

• **Make do with two purses:** one shoulder bag for work and a clutch style for dress.

Sale Calendar

Sale prices average from 10% to 30% off in major department stores. Smaller stores will reduce from 10% to 50% off, but their mark-up is usually higher to begin with. Try to save at least 20%. Be sure to check the store's return policy on sale items.

January: post-holiday sales. Furs, men's suits, coats, dresses, infants' wear, sportswear, shoes, handbags, lingerie, jewelry

February: Washington's Birthday sales. Winter clothes, furs, sportswear

March: winter clothing sales. Children's shoes, infants' wear, hats, hosiery

April: after-Easter and spring sales. Women's shoes, women's and children's coats, men's and boys' suits, dresses, infants' wear, fabric, sleepwear

May: Mother's Day and Memorial Day sales. Handbags, jewelry, lingerie

June: Father's Day sales. Men's and boys' clothing, women's shoes, sleepwear, lingerie, hosiery

July: 4th of July sales. Shoes, hats, furs, fabric, summer sportswear, purses, lingerie, children's clothes

August: back-to-school sales. Summer clothes, coats, furs

September: Labor Day sales. Children's back-to-school specials

October: Columbus Day sales. School clothes, women's coats, fall sportswear

November: Veterans' Day, Election Day, Thanksgiving and pre-Christmas sales. Women's coats, men's suits, dresses, shoes

December: pre- and post-Christmas sales. Women's coats, men's suits, men's and women's shoes, children's clothes, jewelry

Nine-to-five basics for men

There are two basic choices for men when it comes to dressing for their nine-to-five business schedule. One look is the traditional corporate image and the other is a creative image. The corporate image is designed for men in law, banking, insurance and related conservative fields. The creative image includes men in advertising, education, communications, retailing and various people-oriented professions. Both images have their own set of dressing rules, but quality fabric and workmanship are important in each category. Look for "three-season" weight fabrics for maximum wear—you'll probably find you can squeeze four seasons out of garments made from them.

• **To save money on your nine-to-five wardrobe,** shop January retail clearance sales (see page 12), men's designer discount stores and outlets (see pages 73 and 77), men's resale stores (see page 100), or second-hand thrift stores (see page 105).

Corporate image basics for men

• **Choose two suits** of 100% wool or a wool blend, one dark (navy blue or black) and one in a medium color (gray). You can buy two-piece or three-piece suits. However, three-piecers are more expensive, and the current trend is leaning away from the vested suit.

• **Select three shirts.** Either 100% cotton or cotton-blend long sleeve shirts in soft solid colors (white, eggshell, light gray) are best.

• **Invest in a pair of shoes.** Buy one pair of black or brown wing tip or plain tie leather shoes. Wear longer length dark stockings.

• **Pick two conservative ties.** Select at least one tie in a 100% silk fabric.

• **Choose a plain black or brown belt.** Carry a simple leather briefcase.

• **Select an all-weather trench coat** with a zip-out lining.

Creative image basics for men

• **Choose two sportcoats,** one 100% wool Harris Tweed or herringbone pattern coat and

Nine-to-five basics for men

one 100% wool or wool-blend textured, solid color suit. Make sure the trousers of the solid color suit also match the tweed or herringbone sportcoat. Select an extra pair of trousers to match both colors of sportcoats. Good color choices are blue, gray, beige or brown.

• **Select three shirts.** Either 100% cotton or cotton blend button-down collared shirts (white, eggshell, light blue).

• **Pick two ties:** one striped and one textured wool knit.

• **Choose one 100% wool sweater vest** or a V-neck sweater that will match both the suit and the sportcoat.

• **Buy a pair of brown leather loafers,** either tassel style or penny loafers.

• **Select an all-weather trench coat** with a zip-out lining.

Sale Terms in Advertisements

Familiarize yourself with these sale terms to help you determine the type of sale you will be attending.

Sale	The retailer has reduced the price on merchandise regularly sold in the store.
Special Purchase	The retailer has purchased the merchandise at a lower price from the manufacturer and will sell it for a reduced price. Sometimes special purchases are bought just for sales. Be sure that you are not buying poor quality items.
Clearance	This should be regular store merchandise offered at a reduced price to clear it out. It's not a true clearance sale if new merchandise has been brought in for the sale. Question the salespeople about this.
Regularly	If an item is marked "regularly $20.00, now $14.00," the $20.00 price must be what it sold for before the sale.
Comparable Value	This term is used when a retailer puts merchandise on sale that is similar in make and value to regular store merchandise, but not identical. Look for the similarities and differences to determine if the goods really are worth the sale price.
Introductory Offer	This is merchandise that is being sold at a price reduction but will increase later when the item is permanently placed on the market.

(continued)

Sale Terms (continued)

Closeout Sale	If the manufacturer has discontinued making a product, the retailer may reduce the price of the remaining stock.
Warehouse Sale	Merchandise is reduced and sold out of the retailer's warehouse and is not available in his or her store at the reduced price.
Manufacturer's List or Suggested Retail Price	Don't be fooled by the list or suggested price and think you are buying for a great deal less than that price. Knowledge of current prices actually being charged is your real guide to how much you're really saving.
Below Wholesale	The retailer has bought the merchandise for below his wholesale cost and can pass on the saving. Check this merchandise carefully for seconds and irregulars.
Going Out of Business Sale (Liquidation Sale)	The retailer offers sale prices because he or she is going out of business. Be wary of any "going out of business" sale that lasts for months.
Irregular or Second	The words *irregular* and *second* are often confused when they are used in terms of clothing. Clothing must be labeled as to whether it is a second or an irregular. A second is more flawed than an irregular. Often garments marked irregular only have a slight flaw, but be sure to locate the flaw before buying. Sometimes the salesperson can help to find the irregularity. Don't shy away from buying irregulars; just check them carefully.

Stores' wardrobe planning services for women

Most women who work in offices seem to object to wearing tailored suits if it means looking like office clones. However, they *are* interested in dressing appropriately for work, and they want to spend less time and money doing it.

Many major department stores and larger clothing stores in major cities are now offering personal shopping services for women. Jacqueline Ari Murray, director of "For Your Image" at Dayton's in Minneapolis, explains that, although in the past many women looked as though they were wearing an office uniform, it was not the fault of John Molloy, author of *Dress for Success*. Instead, it was the fault of clothing manufacturers who were not making a variety of quality clothes geared to the needs of well-dressed career women. Today, manufacturers are taking an interest in these consumers, and better merchandise with greater variety is now available.

If you are short on time and hate to shop, consider a store's wardrobe planning service. For no charge, you will be helped to plan and buy your wardrobe at a particular store. This benefits the store because you become a full wardrobe customer. Yet if you buy within the framework of your clothing budget, the end result may save you money, especially when you consider the value per wear (see page 10).

Ask for free professional advice on how to buy fewer high-quality clothes and wear them frequently, in a variety of ways, for a longer period of time. That's the formula for investment dressing. However, if you have time to shop around at several stores for bargains and plan your purchases carefully, this service may not be for you.

• **If you live in a large city,** phone a major department store or large clothing store in your area and ask if it offers a wardrobe planning service for women.

• **If you live in a smaller city,** you may want to consider commuting to a larger city in your state for this service. You can go once for an interview, plan your long-range wardrobe needs and have the service mail you your garments.

• **If you have a limited clothing budget,** don't avoid this service just because you feel intimidated. Long-range planning will pay off. You can get assistance purchasing certain items during store clearance sales.

Independent image consultants

You can also get help with wardrobe planning from an independent image consultant. Generally these specialists charge by the hour for their services, which may include appraising what you now own along with guidance on future purchases. Most don't deal with bargain clothing sources (new *or* second-hand), so you must weigh their value to you carefully. They may, however, offer advice on more than just your clothing, from your body language to your speaking manner to your career development. Consider whether they could be helpful to you.

• **Know exactly how the consultant works.** Ask what he or she can or cannot do, what you will be charged and what clothing sources the consultant uses before you begin.

10 Time-Savers for Shoppers

1. Make a list of your wardrobe needs (see page 7).

2. List your driver's license and phone numbers on your checks for quicker service.

3. Shop in season. You'll spend more but you will save time searching.

4. When possible, choose the items you need from store catalogs or mail order catalogs, rather than shopping for them in person.

5. Save time by phoning ahead to locate items and compare prices.

6. Before you leave home, make a last-minute check of your purse or wallet for credit cards, checkbook, shopping list, fabric samples and shopping tools (a calculator, measuring tape, and for second-hand clothes, a pen flashlight, a small mirror, a magnifying glass, and a map if you're unfamiliar with the shopping territory).

7. Shop alone. Children and other adult company will slow you down.

8. Shop during less crowded times, such as weekday mornings and at dinnertime.

9. Ask directions immediately whenever you're unsure of a store layout. When you're really in a hurry, shop familiar territory.

10. Save your store receipts, particularly if you pay with cash. This will save you time later if you need to return the item.

When not to buy

There are times when you really are shopping at a disadvantage. These are not the best times to make a purchase!

• **When you are depressed.** Maybe you feel that buying something will give you a lift. If you need to make an impulse purchase, go to a thrift store rather than a major department store. You can make an inexpensive purchase and feel better.

• **When you spot an item you have been looking for** but unfortunately you don't have the skirt, blouse or whatever to match it. Ask if the store will hold the item, rather than buying it immediately.

• **When you are feeling fat and unattractive,** but need to buy a new bathing suit. Let it wait. You'll just feel frustrated and probably won't buy anything anyway.

• **When you have been on your feet all day** and they are swollen. Don't pick this time to start looking for a pair of shoes!

• **When you must have a dressy outfit for tomorrow night,** *and* you always wind up hating the items you buy in a hurry. You may want to shop for a dressy outfit when there's *no* occasion in sight. Choose a class outfit and then let it wait in your closet until that special occasion arrives. But for tomorrow night, look first in your closet and assemble an outfit from the clothes you've already got. Stretch your imagination... it'll work.

- **When you are feeling rushed into making a purchase** because your children, husband or whoever you're shopping with is tired and crabby and wants to go home.

- **When you find an item that you're not quite sure you like**—or that is not the best quality for the price. Hold off buying.

- **When you're getting ready for a vacation** and you're short on shopping time. Don't try to buy all the items you need before you leave town. Save some of your shopping for your vacation.

Money Angles

Your dollar buys less today than it did yesterday—and who knows what it will buy tomorrow? Does this mean you should spend it right now? No—it means you must know how to stretch your dollar further than you ever did before. Play *all* your money angles. Make your income, no matter what size it is, work for you. In this section you will learn how to increase your spending power, purchase goods without exchanging cash, and safely take a tax credit on the clothes you never wear.

In her book, *Money Dynamics for the 1980's*, money expert Venita Van Caspel says, "Inflation rewards those who owe money, not those who pay cash." Some people misinterpret this type of statement as advocating "plastic money" (credit cards), but this is not her intention. She

When Credit Makes Sense

1. If you spend more money when you carry cash. One charge card would be best for you.

2. If you can avoid paying interest (depending on the type of charge card you have). Buy at the beginning of the billing cycle. You will get an "interest-free" gain of 60 days if you pay the balance in your required time period.

3. If you want to save valuable time by purchasing items by phone or mail order.

4. If you are taking advantage of a sale or a large discount. But remember that the reduced price will still have to be figured against your monthly interest charge.

5. If you travel for business and need the records for tax purposes. In that case use a travel and entertainment card (American Express, Diners Club, Carte Blanche). This type of card, in most cases, will make you pay in 30 days (see page 20). It may also be convenient for you to use if you're out of town and an emergency occurs.

goes on to advise, "Never charge anything you can't pay for in 30 days and never borrow for your daily living or luxuries. Only borrow long term for investing, never for spending." It may be difficult to follow this advice when you are living on a fixed income. However, you will be rewarded financially if you carefully balance your money options with charge cards, loans, and your hard-earned cash.

When There's No Sense to Credit

1. If you do not have a steady source of income.

2. If you buy impulsively when you have credit cards. Consider swaps, bartering and other angles (see pages 24–26).

3. If you don't pay your bills in the month they are due. You don't want to be paying interest on money you already can't afford.

4. If you are worried about stolen credit cards. You can be liable for the first $50.00 charged by the thief. If you have several credit cards stolen, it's $50.00 for each card.

Cash, Credit or Loan?

Clothing is one of the most common items people charge on their credit cards. Before you whip out that easy "plastic money," consider your options. One reminder: interest charges on all loans, even charge accounts, are tax deductible.

Cash	Don't take a large sum of money out of your savings account to buy clothing if you know you will not pay your savings account back monthly. Instead pay the interest on a loan for one year, and continue to earn the interest on your savings.
Credit	Use your credit card if you can pay off your balance in 30 days. Call the store (or check your monthly statement) to determine when your account gets billed. Buy at the *beginning* of the store billing cycle and avoid the interest charge. Also use your credit card if you are tight on cash and have an opportunity to buy something on sale (add the interest to the sale price to judge your real cost).
Loans	A loan from your credit union or bank (even if you have to put up collateral) will cost less in interest than using your bank credit card (Visa or Mastercharge). Check your bank or credit union first before you charge a major wardrobe purchase.

Differences in "Plastic Money"

Bank Credit Cards	These cards (Visa, Mastercharge) are fairly easy to obtain. No interest is charged if you pay your bill in full when you receive it. The interest rate varies from 10% to 24%. Banks usually charge $10.00 to $25.00 a year for these cards.
Travel and Entertainment Cards	These cards (American Express, Diners Club, Carte Blanche) require a higher income and are sometimes difficult to obtain. Normally your payment in full is required when you're billed. You can extend payments on some mail-order items. Interest varies according to the card; the average interest is 12% to 18%. The cost for this type of card varies from $30.00 to $50.00 a year.
Annual Interest Rates	Most retailers charge you an annual interest rate on your charge account balance. The average interest rate varies from 12% to 18% (18% yearly interest charge equals 1.5% monthly interest). Read your charge account agreement carefully and know what interest you will be charged.
Adjusted Balance or Closing Balance Method	This type of charge account gives you the best finance terms on interest. It means that you are charged interest against the remaining balance of the previous month (*if* you have made a payment on the previous month's balance). So you are not paying interest on the full bill from the beginning of that month.
Open 30-Day Account	With this system, you pay your charge account balance in 30 days and don't pay interest.
Revolving Charge	The retailer sets a limit on how high your charge ceiling can reach. The amount is determined by the store, based on your income and ability to pay. On this type of card you are charged monthly interest on the unpaid balance.

(continued)

Differences *(continued)*

Flexible Account   You pay a monthly amount based on the amount owed each month. The more you owe, the more you pay. You are charged monthly interest on the unpaid balance.

Tax Angles

Consider these tax angles and let your clothes go to work for you. Clothes you wear to work which are stipulated by your employer as necessary for your job, or which qualify as uniforms and are only suitable for work, can be written off as a tax deduction. Be sure to keep your receipts. Clothes you donate to charitable institutions can also be claimed for a tax benefit. (But note that items you buy at charitable institutions are *not* tax deductible, because you have received merchandise in exchange for your donation.)

Taking the credit

You can deduct the Fair Market Value of each item of clothing you donate to charitable organizations from your income when you figure your taxes. You cannot, however, claim the money you *spend* on clothes at church or other charitable sales as donations. Here's what you can do:

• **Before you drop off your old clothes,** list the items and their Fair Market Value (what you could get somebody to pay for them—approximately garage sale prices), plus their ages: 1 brown men's suit, 5 years old, $10.00. (See page 110 for sample garage sale prices.) Get the person who receives your clothes for the charity to sign and date your list and keep it as a receipt with your tax records.

• **If you drop things off at a collection box,** your unsigned list will still be an acceptable receipt. Or you can write to the charity for a form on which you can list the items—but that's not strictly necessary.

• **If you're not sure about Fair Market Values,** ask your drycleaner to appraise things for you. He or she should be very familiar with rates.

Profit Angles

You can make money on the clothes you're not going to wear by selling them at garage sales or at a resale (consignment) store. You can also make money if you buy second-hand vintage clothing and resell the items to a vintage clothing store (see pages 111–112). The demand is high for clothes from the 20's to the 50's and for special items that are current fads.

There are people who are professionals at this resale game. They pick through every garage sale, rummage sale, thrift store and Salvation Army store, buying vintage clothing for 50¢ and

75¢. Then they resell items to the resale and antique stores for three times that amount.

Some areas of the country are more profitable for these pros than others. In major cities (New York, Chicago, San Francisco and Los Angeles), it's difficult to find yesterday's threads for resale. But you can find a garage sale or apartment sale anywhere —here's how a neighbor and I put on a terrific garage sale last summer.

We decided to have some fun along with the work! I hired a friend to play guitar and sing for $50.00 for the day and first pick of the merchandise. The week before the sale, we phoned everyone we knew and invited them to a "live music garage sale." Then we put an ad in the local newspaper (cost of the ad: $18.00). We also scattered signs around the neighborhood on the evening before the sale.

Our sale items included clothing (priced from 50¢ to $8.00), a few books and a table of knickknacks. Our total sales for the day were $589.00; my profit (after sharing expenses) came to $245.00. I made some money and we all had an entertaining afternoon of music and bargaining! Read on to see how you can do it too.

Garage sales

Garage sales are almost pure profit—if you don't count your time and labor in conducting them!

• **Planning.** Conduct your own garage sale or hold a sale with a friend. You don't need a garage to have a sale—even a small apartment will suffice.

• **Advertising.** To announce your sale, put signs up in the neighborhood. Telephone poles are a convenient spot! Place an ad in your neighborhood newspaper. Remember that spring and fall weekends are best.

• **Displaying.** Hang your clothes neatly on racks; they'll sell better that way. If you run out of hangers, fold as little as possible on tables. Place jewelry and accessories on a colorful cloth.

• **Tagging.** Tag all clothing, shoes and accessories individually (initial the tag if it's a joint sale). Put the sizes on the price tags too. This is especially important with men's clothing.

• **Pricing.** Price the clothes to sell, but consider in doing so an item's condition, current styling, present market value and how badly you want to get rid of it. Place a higher price on current clothes of 100% cottons, wools or silks. Here are some price suggestions for clothes in good condition:

men's suits—$15.00 to $25.00
men's sportcoats—$12.00 to $18.00
men's slacks—$10.00 to $12.00
men's shirts—$3.00 to $5.00
ties and belts—$1.00 to $2.00
men's and women's sweaters—$2.00 to $8.00
men's and women's shoes—$2.00 to $8.00
women's blazers—$5.00 to $15.00

women's dresses and skirts—$3.00 to $10.00
blouses—$1.00 to $6.00
slacks—$3.00 to $8.00
accessories, purses and jewelry—under $5.00
children's play clothes— 25¢ to $5.00
children's dressy clothes— $1.00 to $8.00

Flea markets

The advantage of a flea market is the large number of potential buyers who attend. You'll also save the cost of a newspaper ad. The disadvantages are the rental fee and the nuisance of hauling your merchandise to the market.

• **Ads.** Look in your newspaper want ads, under *Miscellaneous Sales*, for locations of flea markets that run every weekend.

• **Fees.** Check out the rental fee for a small space. An average price is $25.00 a day, but it should be cheaper per day if you rent for two days. If you don't have enough clothing to make the fee worthwhile, ask a friend to join you.

• **Displays.** Bring a clothes rack (tables are usually provided). Size and price each item.

• **Pricing.** Use the garage-sale clothing prices as a guide. Leave a slight margin for bargaining.

• **Tools.** Keep a measuring tape and medium-size mirror handy for your customers.

Resale (consignment) stores

If you decide to sell your clothes through a resale shop, you'll save time and energy, but your profits will be less than if you sold the clothes on your own.

• **Locating resale stores.** Look in your phone book's yellow pages under *Second-Hand Stores, Thrift Stores, Men's Apparel* or *Women's Apparel* to locate a resale store near you.

• **Policies.** Phone the store and ask about their policies. What percentage profit does the store take? Most stores take a 50% profit from the sale of your clothes; you get the other 50%. When are their "clothing take-in times"? Do they have any condition or style requirements?

• **What to sell.** Bring in clothes that are clean and in season, but don't be afraid to show *all* your rejects and let the store decide what will sell.

Buying to resell

I know a woman who makes her living by combing through rummage sales and thrift stores, and then reselling her finds to antique and consignment shops! Here are her secrets.

• **Study up.** Know the styles of vintage clothing (see pages 143–147), and get a feel for old fabrics (rayon, silk, gabardine). Watch old movies on television to familiarize yourself with the fashions of past eras.

• **Locate stores.** Look in the yellow pages under *Antiques,*

Clothing and *Second-Hand Stores* to find vintage specialty stores in your area. Visit the stores and look over the merchandise. Ask the owner or manager if the store buys clothes from private parties. Find out what types of clothing they need.

• **Research prices.** Pick items out of the store stock and ask what you would be paid for the item if you had brought it in to sell. This will aid you in figuring your profit margin, and it can tell you how much money you should spend for the item originally.

• **Find clothes.** Shop for clothes at garage sales, thrift stores, auctions, rummage sales, Salvation Army stores and Goodwill stores. Invest an amount that will return three times your cost.

• **Move fast.** Hit the sales early. Other people will be doing the same thing you are.

• **Get prime choices.** Choose items in good condition and in average sizes; they will be the easiest to resell.

• **Getting stuck.** Don't worry about being stuck with the clothes. If you can't sell them to a store, you can donate them (for a tax deduction) or hold a garage sale. After all, your investment is minimal.

• **Prices.** Don't be greedy: $2.25 may not seem like much to be paid, compared to what the antique or vintage store will sell the item for, but keep in mind the fact that you are making a 200% profit on your dollar.

Cashless Angles

Today's inflation has spurred new interest in an old idea—bartering. More and more people are swapping goods and services instead of their hard-earned cash.

You can do it too. You can swap your merchandise for someone else's merchandise. For example, a church in my neighborhood runs a swap shop for children's clothes. Every Saturday afternoon, people come in with clothing that no longer fits their children and exchange it for clothing that will fit. You can start a similar swap shop in your own community, or call local private schools to see if one already exists.

How to barter

If you're interested in swapping your services or goods, these tips will help you begin.

• **Survey your options.** Make a list of the types of services you could barter for merchandise: cleaning, outdoor work, typing, bookkeeping, child care. Keep an open, imaginative mind to the talents you may have to exchange.

• **Call professionals** who perform the services you can provide. Ask what they charge and use this information as a guide to what you will "charge."

• **Look for bartering partners.** Talk to your neighbors first. They may be willing to barter, or they may know somebody else who'd be interested.

• **Advertise.** Put an ad in your community newspaper want ads. You can word it like this: "I will swap my services of typing, cleaning or car washing for good condition boys' clothing, size 4." Or you may want to put in an ad to swap your clothes for someone else's. It could read: "I will swap men's suits, size 40 regular, for women's suits, size 12."

• **Visit small, privately owned stores** that carry the type of merchandise you're looking for. Offer the person in charge services in exchange for clothing. If you don't get anywhere, question the person about the store's needs. You may even be able to offer a service you hadn't originally considered.

• **Name terms.** No matter who you barter with, settle on the terms of your exchange explicitly. A fair agreement is one that both parties feel comfortable doing.

• **Tax angles.** In some cases this cashless system is considered taxable income by the Internal Revenue Service. Exchanges with non-business people (friends or neighbors) for goods and services are not taxable. If you trade your professional services for professional goods from a store, however, it is taxable income.

Bargaining Techniques

During times of inflation, no matter where you shop, prices on expensive items (furs, jewelry and so on) are usually negotiable. Smaller stores, unable to keep large inventories, sometimes show more readiness to bargain on less expensive items. So it pays to learn to be a good bargainer.

Negotiate the best price

Here are some tips to get you warmed up. (Chapters 4 and 5 include bargaining techniques designed for specific clothing sources, both new and second-hand.)

• **Make sure** the salesperson you intend to bargain with has the power to make a price reduction.

• **Be polite.** Keep your sense of humor and don't ever put the salesperson in a position of losing face.

• **Know the current market prices** on the item you want. If a store is more expensive than its competitor, ask if the store can meet the competitor's price.

• **Ask if an item will be going on sale,** and if so, ask if it can be sold *now* for the sale price.

• **Offer cash or a check** instead of a charge card and inquire if you can get a reduction on the item for saving the merchant his service charge. This often works in small stores that don't offer their own charge accounts.

- **Pick out a second item** and add it to the merchandise you're bargaining on. If there's no negotiating on the price of the original item, ask if the second item could be thrown in for no additional cost. This works well when buying second-hand at garage sales, thrift stores and rummage sales.

- **Group several items together.** Ask the salesperson if they will take a fixed amount for the whole group of items. Again, this method works well with second-hand goods.

- **Bargain about a flaw** whenever you're buying second-hand. Point the flaw out and ask, "How much would you be willing to come down for this?"

- **Reaching an impasse.** If there's no negotiating on price, be sure to thank the person and leave. But if you're at a rummage sale and the price hasn't budged, buy it anyway if you still want it. You're still likely to leave with a good deal in hand!

Quick Shopping Route for a Budget Wardrobe

You can systematically work your way through one shopping day into a budget wardrobe. Follow this shopping route. You'll be starting at the lowest price sources and working your way up. This will keep your clothing expenses low. Remember that this system works best when you know the current prices of all these sources. Then you can spot a really good deal at each source. By the time you hit the most expensive source, you may have only a few items left to buy. Your closet appraisal (see pages 3–8) will tell you what items you've already got and what new pieces you'll need. Remember to bring your list along with you!

- **1st stop:** thrift stores.

- **2nd stop:** resale (consignment) stores.

- **3rd stop:** designer discount or outlet stores.

- **4th stop:** sample shops.

- **5th stop:** discount shoe stores.

- **6th stop:** major retail department stores.
  Go to one with a bargain basement and comb it first before you go upstairs.

Recognizing Bargains When You See Them

The buyer who can recognize a well-made garment has a shopping edge at every retail sale, discount store or second-hand source—a little clothing knowledge goes a long way to save you time and money. This chapter will give you the education in quality clothes that you'll need to spot a real bargain when you see it. You'll learn the difference between a classic style and a fad, discover what fabrics perform well and become familiar with the signs of good workmanship.

Bring this book with you when you're shopping for a bargain. Use it as a handy guide to help you get the best quality for your money.

Quality Construction

Designer labels are only one indication of quality clothing (and even they can occasionally lead you astray). There are certain distinctive features in a well-constructed garment. Egon Von Furstenberg advises men to try on the most expensive suits at fine clothing stores before buying at any price. In *The Power Look*, he says, "having tried the best, you will be better able to achieve the best look at any price." This advice is good for both men and women. If you do

this before you shop at any discount or second-hand clothing sources, examining how expensive clothing is constructed, then you can inspect clothes you buy for less with a critical, knowledgeable eye.

Quality workmanship

Look for these quality indicators as a "first glance" guide.

• **Good fabric.** Choose pure natural fabrics or fabrics with a good percentage blend of both natural and synthetic fibers (see pages 32–33).

• **Tightly woven fabric,** since it will perform longer than a loosely woven fabric. Hold the material up to a light. The tighter the weave, the less the light will shine through the fabric.

• **Patterns, plaids and stripes that match up** at the seams and armholes.

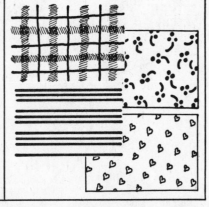

- **Neat, even stitches** along seams, behind collars and at the edges of pockets.

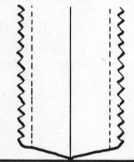

- **Inside seams that are well finished:** stitched at the edge or cut with a pinking shears to prevent unraveling.

- **A generous center back seam** in men's trousers, which comes in handy if you need to make alterations later.

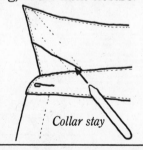

- **Removable collar stays** in shirts. A good shirt will also have a reinforced fabric (interfacing) at the front closure.

Collar stay

- **Flat-felled seams** on jeans, work clothes and children's play clothes (this is a seam with two rows of stitching showing on the outside of clothes). A flat-felled seam is more durable than a plain seam.

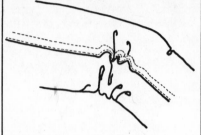

- **Double stitching** around armholes for reinforcement.

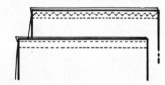

- **Buttonholes** that fit the button tightly. Better-quality clothes manufacturers use good buttons. Look for buttons made of mother of pearl, wood or brass.

- **Collars** on men's jackets and women's blazers that have a felt backing underneath the collar. This will help retain the collar shape.

Felt backing

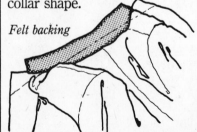

Quality Construction Guide

The more you know, the easier it is to spot a bargain! This is especially true when you are shopping second-hand. Often labels are cut out or are missing from clothing. Or you're shopping under the pressures of a frantic rummage sale. Study this construction guide to improve your bargain-hunting knowledge.

Buttonholes	Make sure buttons slide easily through the holes. Buttonhole corners should be reinforced with thread, showing no fraying edges. Check for even spacing between the buttonholes.
Collars	A wool or wool-blend jacket should have a collar with a flat flannel lining on the opposite side. This will help retain a good fit around the neck and chest.
Hems	The hem width should be ample enough to allow for lengthening and the hem should hang evenly. Stitching should not show through to the right side of the material.
Lining	Lining works best when it is hemmed to the bottom of a jacket, blazer or sportcoat. It may be attached to a coat vent or at several points at the side seams. Lining does not wear well when it is completely attached or sewn to the entire coat fabric because the friction of movement will cause strain on the garment. You can check to see how the lining is attached by pulling the lining to see if it moves easily away from the fabric.
Reinforcement	Any extra reinforcement in children's clothing is a plus. This will help add extra life to the garment. Clothing designed for rugged use should be double-stitched at the seams. Look for double stitching or patches at points of strain: underarms, crotches, elbows, knees.
Seams	Seams should lie flat with no signs of puckering or unraveling. There should be enough seam width to withstand strain. Half an inch is the average width

(continued)

Quality Construction *(continued)*

	for natural fabrics; synthetics require more width.
Stitching	There should be no hanging threads on a garment. Look for stitches that are small and threads that do not pull or pucker. Topstitching on collars, pockets and edges should be straight. The thread ought to be a good color match for the fabric. Transparent plastic thread is a cheap substitute, because it will pull out easily and is a sign of poor workmanship.
Interfacing	Interfacing is the extra material added to lapels, collars and fronts of suit jackets and cuffs to help them retain their shape. Check for puckering in the interfacing areas of the garment. Shoulder pads should be soft and smoothly shaped with no puckering at the back of the shoulder or armholes.
Zippers	Zippers should lie flat and straight and have a cover (overlap) of material. Check to see if the zipper slides easily. When the zipper is closed, pull on it to make sure it stays closed.

Quality Fabric

Your fabric choice in a garment is critical for the following reasons: the correct fabric will drape well, hold its shape, wear longer and clean properly. Fabric can make a difference in whether a garment looks classy or just ordinary.

Your knowledge of good fabric will lead you to clothes that will save you money, will be easy to take care of and will make you look and feel great. This section can help you determine which fabrics will perform well for you. Then when you've developed the feel for good material, you can select the best value for your money, new or second-hand.

Natural and synthetic fibers

There are basically two types of fibers, natural (wool, cotton, silk) and man-made or synthetic (polyester, rayon, nylon). It's important to read fabric labels and know what you're buying. Any fiber content over 5% must, by law, be listed on all clothing.

Today the trend is away from the synthetics and polyesters and back to the 100% natural fibers, or to natural and synthetic blends. A garment with a label that says it's made of 100% natural wool, silk or cotton, or even a good blend of natural and synthetic fibers, can be one measure of a quality item. In looking for quality clothing, you must also know yourself and what type of demands you will put on the material you choose. Remember to ask yourself how much effort you want to put into maintaining the fabric you choose.

• **Check to see if a fabric will wrinkle easily** before you buy. Place the fabric in your palm and squeeze; then let go. The material should spring back to shape and not stay wrinkled.

Wool

Wool fabrics are made of new, reprocessed or used wool.

• **New or virgin wool** is made totally from new or virgin fibers and has never been woven before. Look for this sign when buying new or virgin wool.

PURE WOOL

• **Reprocessed wool** is wool that has never been worn, but is made of left-over scraps, pulled apart and rewoven. Reprocessed wool fibers may get damaged in the process, and so this fabric is of a lower quality than new wool.

• **Reused wool** is recycled wool from garments that have been worn by consumers, then broken down into a fibrous form

and remade into a new garment. Reused wool is of the lowest quality.

What a fiber blend can do for you

Synthetic fibers can be woven into easy-care material that is a real timesaver, though the fabric is not very luxurious in look and feel. Natural fabrics are often more time-consuming and expensive to maintain, but they look and feel great. Synthetics blended with natural fibers can combine the good points of each type of fiber.

• **Polyester** added to cotton and wool gives strength, crease resistance and shrink resistance.

• **Rayon** added to cotton gives luster.

• **Acrylic** added to wool provides strength, crease resistance and shrink resistance.

• **Acrylic** added to cotton gives crease resistance, shrink resistance, minimum ironing, fast drying and softness.

• **Acetate** added to cotton supplies a smooth touch and a more luxurious look.

• **Nylon** added to wool, rayon, cotton or acetate provides strength, pleat retention, spot resistance, shrink resistance, fast drying and minimum ironing.

WOOL BLEND

Natural Fibers

Fiber	Characteristics	Assets	Liabilities	Typical Garments
Cotton (pique, cotton jersey, oxford cloth)	Sturdy, smooth, absorbent, versatile	Excellent to wash and wear, colorfast	Wrinkles easily, weakens in sunlight	Blouses, men's shirts, children's clothing
Linen (flax)	Crisp looking, nubby texture	Dries quickly, lint free, cool to wear	Poor wrinkle resistance, can be itchy, hand wash	Dresses, suits, hand towels
Silk (organza, crepe, chiffon)	Soft, smooth, luxurious, drapes well on the body	Strong fiber, dyes easily, lightweight holds shape	Needs extra care, perspiration stains will rot fabric	Blouses, dresses, drapery
Wool				
Worsted (gabardine, worsted flannel, sharkskin)	Smooth, firm, longer fiber	More durable than woolen, holds shape well, fabric tailors easily	Some have allergies to worsted wool, not moth-proof	Women's suits, men's suits
Woolen (merino wool, wool flannel, tweed, wool shetland; can be sheer—crepes—or heavy in garments)	Shorter fiber, softer than worsted	Durable, wrinkles will hang out, slow to show soil, warm, comfortable to most	Some have allergies to wool, most wool needs dry cleaning or hand washing	Sweaters, men's and women's suits

Man-Made Fibers

Fiber	Characteristics	Assets	Liabilities	Typical Garments
Acetate (Arnel, Celanese, Triacetate)	Silk-like, soft, drapes well	Good wrinkle resistance, good crease retention	Some dyes will fade, dry cleaning recommended (nail polish remover will dissolve acetate)	Lingerie; knitted fabrics in sportswear for men, women and children; used as lining for coats and jackets
Acrylic (Acrilan, Creslan, Orlon)	Soft, similar to wool, has a shinier look	Dyes well; resistant to sunlight, moths; blends well with other fibers	Has a tendency to stretch out of shape	Sweaters, knitwear for men and women, fake fur fabrics, blankets
Nylon (Antron, Quiana, Zeflon)	Silky, slippery, knit nylon is stretchable	Colorfast, does not shrink, strong, lightweight, washes easily, dries quickly	White nylon will turn gray; nylon must be washed separately	Lingerie, hosiery, stretch fabric, carpeting
Polyester (Dacron, Fortrel, Kodel, Trevira)	Slippery, some shine in fabric	Resistant to wrinkling, blends well with other fabrics, machine wash and dry	Care must be taken with stains before they set	Suits, slacks for men and women, children's clothing
Rayon (Avisco, Avril, Coloray)	Shiny slippery	Strong, attractive, versatile, blends well	Must use low-iron temperature	Lingerie, blouses, sportswear, dresses

Fabric Blends for Easy Care

Note: In a permanent-pleated skirt of synthetic material, the blend must be at least 55% or more nylon, arnel or polyester to retain the permanent pleat and to have ease of care. In a permanent-pleated skirt of 100% wool, remember that you must dryclean the fabric, rather than use home care.

Blend	Garment	Minimum Percentage
Rayon with cotton	T-shirts, knitwear	40–68% cotton
Acetate with cotton	Sportswear	30–50% cotton
Nylon with cotton	Work clothes	15–20% cotton
Polyester (e.g., Dacron) with cotton	Shirts	35–50% cotton
Polyester (e.g., Kodel) with rayon	Shirts, slacks	35–50% rayon
Polyester (e.g., Fortrel) with wool	Suits	45–55% wool
Acrylic with worsted wool	Suits, slacks sportswear	30–50% worsted wool
Acrylic with woolen	Slacks, suits, coats	30–50% woolen
Orlon with wool	Suits	25–35% wool
Orlon with rayon	Sportswear, slacks	25–35% rayon

A Proper Fit

Most of us do not have perfectly proportioned bodies, and I suspect that if we did have model proportions, we still wouldn't be satisfied. I've always been told how lucky I am to have a long neck. Personally, I've found it a disadvantage when I want to wear a blouse with a Peter Pan collar or have my hair cut very short.

If you wish, you can choose the proper clothing to camouflage your body shape. You're simply creating an illusion to cover the problem.

A proper fit in clothing is a combination of clothing illusion with the proper construction and shape for your body. You can find the clothing lines that will work best for you.

Know your body shape

• **Know yourself.** Using a full-length mirror, examine yourself in the nude. I know it's tough, but take a good, honest look. This will help you to know your body shape.

• **Evaluate yourself.** Determine your personal assets and liabilities. Do you have a long neck? Long legs? Short waist?

• **Examine your wardrobe's fit.** Try on clothes from your wardrobe. Do this one piece at a time (jackets, sweaters, vests, slacks). Examine how each item looks on your body shape. What looks best on you?

What Do the Sizes Mean?

Clothing manufacturers recognize that there are lots of figure types to be fitted (or misfitted) in their designs. Here are the conventional definitions for the figure types and their size groups.

Misses' sizes (4, 6, 8, 10, 12, 14, 16, 18, 20, 22)	Average figure types, 5'3" to about 5'6½". Petite Miss heights are under 5'3"; Tall Miss heights go to about 5'11".
Juniors' Sizes (3, 5, 7, 9, 11, 13, 15, 17)	Smaller frames with higher, firmer busts and buttocks, shorter torsos and longer legs than Misses' sizes. Petite and Tall Juniors heights run about the same as Misses.
Women's Sizes (36, 38, 40, 42, 44, 46, 48, 50, 52)	Fuller, rounder, more mature figure with lower bustline; longer from shoulder to waist than Half Sizes. Height is 5'4" to 5'6½".
Half Sizes (14½, 16½, 18½, 20½, 22½, 24½, 26½)	Like the Women's figure type, but shorter from shoulder to the waist than Women's. Height is under 5'4".
Men's Average*	Average figures with about 6 inches difference ("drop") between chest and waist measurements. Heights range between 5'7" and 6'1".
Men's Athlete*	Slim figures with about an 8-inch drop between chest and waist measurements.
Men's Portly*	Figures with little or no drop between chest and waist.

*Men's clothes are also made in variable lengths of sleeve and inseam, which creates many complex combinations such as Athlete Extra Longs (a Marlboro man) or Portly Extra Extra Longs (a tall Orson Welles).

A Fitting and Proper Guide for Women

Suit Jackets and Coats	Jackets and coats should hang straight from the shoulder to the hem. They should fit smoothly over other clothing (blazers, shirts, sweaters, vests). The collar ought to lie flat against the back of the neck. A coat's sleeve should hit the wrist bone when the arm is bent. A jacket's sleeve should fall at the wrist bone. A full-length coat should cover your skirt length. When trying on coats or jackets, swing your arms backward and forward to test for a comfortable fit.
Skirts	Skirts should fit smoothly across the seat and tummy, with no pulling or wrinkling. Pleats in skirts ought to hang straight and closed when you are standing. The waistband should hold the skirt in place, but not so tight that it's uncomfortable and pulls out of shape. Don't be lazy about changing a hem to the current fashion length.
Dresses	If you are buying a belted dress, make sure the waist hits your natural waistline, not above or below. In a dress with a fitted bodice, the vertical waist-to-bustline darts should end right at the tip of the bust. If you are buying a vintage dress with side darts at the bustline, they should fit the center of the breast and end at the tip of the breast. Also check the shoulders of the dress. They should not droop past the end of your own shoulder, unless the dress is designed with a dropped shoulder.
Slacks	Slacks should fit comfortably in the crotch area—never hanging below, but never so tight that the seat area is pulled. This will give the slacks a "cupping" appearance across the buttocks. Make sure the pockets are lying flat, not pulled or gaping open. "Baggy" slacks should be loose around the hips and tum-

(continued)

Fitting Guide *(continued)*

my. The pleats are not meant to be filled out, but to hang loose. If you are short-waisted, don't choose a high-waisted pair of slacks with a wide waistband. This will just shorten your appearance. Cuff slacks and straight-leg slacks should not be angled at the hem. This is true also for slacks that you wear with a higher heel. Angle the hem slightly on slacks worn with flats or cowboy boots. On most slacks, the front hem length should just hit the top of your shoe, letting the slack hang straight with no breaking.

Dressing for Your Figure Type

Short Women

- Choose small patterns.
- Stay in the same color family.
- Pick simple, classic clothing lines.
- Avoid ruffles, fussy detail and bulky styles.

Tall Women

- Contrast your colors. Wear a light top with a dark skirt.
- Avoid fussy looks: elegance is your best bet.
- Designer clothes may best fit your height.
- Wear heels if you like.

Thin Women

- Choose blouses with pleated fronts or other types of detail.
- Choose slacks with front pleats.
- Avoid vertical stripes and elongating narrow lines.
- Pick shoes with a medium heel.

Heavy Women

- Choose clothing that fits well: not loose, hanging looks.
- Wear straight-leg slacks.
- Wear bright colors in the same color family.
- Pick medium-sized accessories in handbags and jewelry.

A Fitting and Proper Guide for Men

Suits	There are two shoulder shapes in suits for men, the *natural* (soft shape) and the *European* (roped, squared-off shape). The natural shape has a minimum of padding. This type of suit fits a more muscular build and a heavier frame. The European cut is more heavily padded and fits more snugly around the arm-holes. The chest area fits tighter, and the waist is nipped in slightly. This type of suit best fits a slimmer body shape.
Jackets	There should be no rippling of material when the jacket is buttoned. The jacket should be smooth across the back from shoulder to shoulder. The collar fit should show ½ to ¾ inch of the shirt collar at the back of the neck. Average lapel width ranges from 3 to 4 inches wide. To determine the proper length for the jacket, check the waist and make sure it corresponds with your own waist. If so, the jacket will fall at the correct point at the bottom. It's important that the sleeve length can allow the cuff of the shirt to show. The proper amount of shirt showing below the sleeve depends on the length of your arms and the size of your hands. If you have long arms or large hands, show only a ¼-inch of cuff. If you have short arms and small hands, allow a ½-inch cuff to show.
Jacket Vents	*Center Vents*: these are seen on natural shoulder jackets. They allow the typical American male shape (larger in the hips than European) more freedom of movement. The vent should lie flat when you're standing still. *Side Vents*: these are commonly used in European jackets. They are less flattering to fuller figured men but work very well on a slimmer figure. There should not be any gaping in the side vents; they should lie flat.

(continued)

Fitting Guide *(continued)*

	Ventless: this type of vent is shown mostly in European jacket styles. Again, this is not for the fuller, muscular male. The ventless jacket fits snugly around the hips and waist, and it is balanced by the broad shoulders.
Trousers	Trousers should fit well across the stomach, hips and rear. They should be comfortable and not pull in the crotch. The fit should not be tight over the thighs and calves. The pant leg should hang straight from the waist with a slight break of fabric on the top of your shoe (no more than ½ inch). The average trouser width at the hem is 19–20 inches. Cuffs on trousers should measure about 1¼–1½ inches in width; they should not break at the top of the shoe but be level with it.

Dressing for Your Figure Type

Short Men

- Avoid sharp, contrasting colors.
- Wear solid-color suits.
- Choose textured fabrics or vertical stripes of medium width.
- Avoid long vests; they'll have a shortening effect.

Tall Men

- Wear contrasting colors, rather than solids.
- Double-breasted suits will help add width.
- Bright shirts with ties that aren't too narrow will take attention away from your height.

Thin Men

- Avoid big sweaters; too much bulk can over-emphasize thinness.
- Don't pick suits with vertical stripes or narrow pin stripes.

Heavy Men

- Stay away from sportcoats.
- For a sports jacket and pants outfit, stick to the same color family. Choose dark, cool colors and a single-breasted suit.
- Subtle designs work best.

Fashion Awareness

Fashion awareness is being familiar with top designer names, recognizing classic styling and choosing a wardrobe staple that will last for several seasons. I enhance my know-how each season by looking through fashion magazines (see page 153). I do this not because I feel we should be slaves to fashion advice, but because I can use this information to my advantage in bargain shopping.

Educate yourself by reading the fashion magazines and newspaper ads; then browse through the better stores. Examine the merchandise, and note how the mannequins are dressed. Familiarize yourself with the style characteristics of various designers.

How to recognize quality designers

Designer jeans have made names like Calvin Klein, Sasson and Jordache household words. Every time I pick up an article of clothing, I look at the manufacturer's label. This keeps me familiar with the top quality designers. I rely on labels and styling characteristics when I am second-hand and discount shopping too.

This familiarity is a great asset at a designer discount store like Loehmann's or Marshall's, where sometimes only part of a designer label is cut out—if you know your labels you can still tell who designed the garment. But when the label is completely cut out, you can often identify the designer by the RN or WPL code number. Each manufacturer is issued, according to federal law, a specific number. This number is usually located near the care label at the collar, on an inside seam or on a hang tag on the sleeve.

There's a book available with all the manufacturers' code numbers. The cost is high— $75.00—but several people could pitch in to buy it together. I've listed the codes for the most popular designer labels. Take the list along to use as a guide the next time you find a label cut out.

In some cases, stores will sew their private label in clothes; they do this for a variety of reasons. First, it keeps other retail competition from recognizing their buying source. Second, the store assumes the customer will become familiar with their name. But the most important reason: the use of private store labels allows the retailer to get a better markup on the clothing. They don't have this option with name brands, which are generally sold for close to the same price everywhere. When a retailer is going to use store labels, they usually make sure the clothing is a quality item. After all, their name is an endorsement.

Deansgate is the name of a clothing manufacturer that not only makes quality items under the Deansgate label (see page 42), but also for retailers to use for a private label (such as Brooks Brothers or Nord-

Designer Code List

When the label is cut out of a garment, use the code to determine the designer. Look for the RN or WPL code numbers, usually located near the care label (or on the union label). (Starred manufacturers also make women's clothes.)

Women's Wear

Abe Schrader RN 15579
Anne Fogarty RN 48648, RN 30669
Anne Klein RN 40803
Beene Bazaar RN 42960
Bonnie Cashin WPL 10113
Calvin Klein RN 41327, RN 42642
Donkenny RN 43594
Evan Picone RN 35685, WPL 08582
Fredericksport WPL 06168
Harvé-Benard RN 40679
Herman Marcus RN 32121
Howard B. Wolf WPL 12324
J.G. Hook RN 51898
Leslie Fay RN 43857, RN 42711, RN 16890
Lilli Ann RN 29563, RN 14962
Lilly Pulitzer RN 39805
Liz Claiborne RN 52002
Oleg Cassini RN 32203, WPL 09352
St. Tropez RN 55862
St. Tropez Swimwear RN 53466
Ms. Sero Shirtmakers RN 17244

Children's Wear

Florence Eiseman RN 17652
★ Izod RN 21008

Men's Wear

★ Bill Blass RN 38344
Botany RN 33734, RN 34313
Burberry RN 31750, RN 44241
Calvin Klein RN 54718
Chaps RN 45408
Corbin WPL 10699
Country Britches RN 44270, RN 44425
★ Deansgate RN 40301, RN 45773
★ Gant RN 16157
Geoffrey Beene RN 33293
Haggar WPL 00386, WPL 11685, WPL 12273
Halston RN 49619
Hart, Schaffner and Marx RN 37207, WPL 04001, WPL 04002
Hickey Freeman RN 55075, RN 55077
Jacques Bellini RN 47109, RN 34686, RN 51450, RN 52121
Jantzen RN 37966
Jaymer-Ruby WPL 00327
Johnny Carson RN 43209, RN 43211
Lacoste WPL 1100
Levi's WPL 00423, RN 36665
★ London Fog RN 47396, RN 47398, RN 47400
Lord Braxton RN 48238
Manhattan RN 44738, WPL 01689
Oleg Cassini WPL 09352
Palm Beach WPL 04224, RN 41599, WPL 03133
★ Pendelton RN 29685, WPL 04378
Pierre Cardin RN 41858
Ralph Lauren (Polo) RN 41381
Rubin Bros. RN 14352
Rubin Bros. Int. RN 50407, RN 20407, RN 51778
San Remo RN 35297
★ Stanley Blacker RN 55639, RN 30219, RN 41550, WPL 11388, WPL 11390
★ Woolrich WPL 06635
Yves St. Laurent RN 48545
Shirts RN 48743

The above listing is from the *RN & WPL Directory,* available from Textile Publishing Corporation, Box 50079, Washington, D.C., (202)-248-5000. Cost: $75.00.

strom's). So you may find the exact same suit at various shops, bearing each store's label, and sold at different prices. It may save you as much as $50.00 to $100.00, if you do comparison pricing on store labels at other shops. Inspect the outfit carefully; memorize the styling detail and fabric content. Your keen eye will give you the shopping edge to save money.

To increase your fashion awareness even more, examine the drawings of designer labels. This knowledge will help when you are trying to identify part of a label or when you are looking for quality in styling.

How to Recognize the Classics

Just what is a fashion classic? That's an important question. When you have the answer, you have a new and second-hand shopping advantage (see page 94). Acquire expertise in spotting a classic. It will save you money because you'll be buying a long-term fashion investment. Also, no matter what you paid for the garment, new or second-hand, you will look as though you spent much more! Now let's try to answer that important question.

Classic lines

These lines are basically clean-cut, simple and middle of the road—no extremes. The classic lines will carry through several seasons. When a classic does need updating, it will be less expensive to alter because of its simple styling.

• **Men's shirts:** white, cream or light blue Oxford shirts (button-down collar).

- **Blouses:** Oxford shirts (button-down collar), silk or polyester/silk tie-front blouses, shawl collars, Peter-Pan collars, stand-up collars and notched collars.

Stand-up collar

Button-down collar

Notched collar

Tie-front collar

Shawl collar

- **Sweaters:** cable-stitched turtlenecks, V-necks, crew necks and cardigans.

Cable-stitched cardigan

Peter-Pan collar

• Skirts: A-line skirts, moderately full dirndls, basic straight skirts.

• Coats: trench or reefer style, double-breasted, camel-colored Chesterfield coats with blazer collars, pea coats.

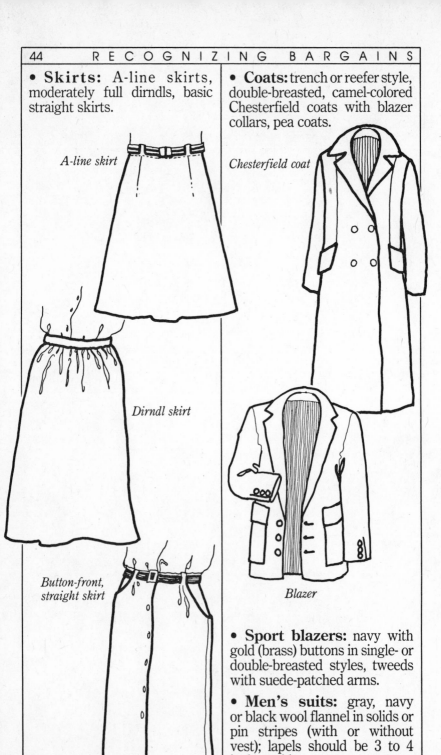

A-line skirt

Chesterfield coat

Dirndl skirt

Button-front, straight skirt

Blazer

• Sport blazers: navy with gold (brass) buttons in single- or double-breasted styles, tweeds with suede-patched arms.

• Men's suits: gray, navy or black wool flannel in solids or pin stripes (with or without vest); lapels should be 3 to 4 inches wide.

- **Slacks:** pleat-front pants, straight-leg pants, corduroys and jeans.

Corduroy pants

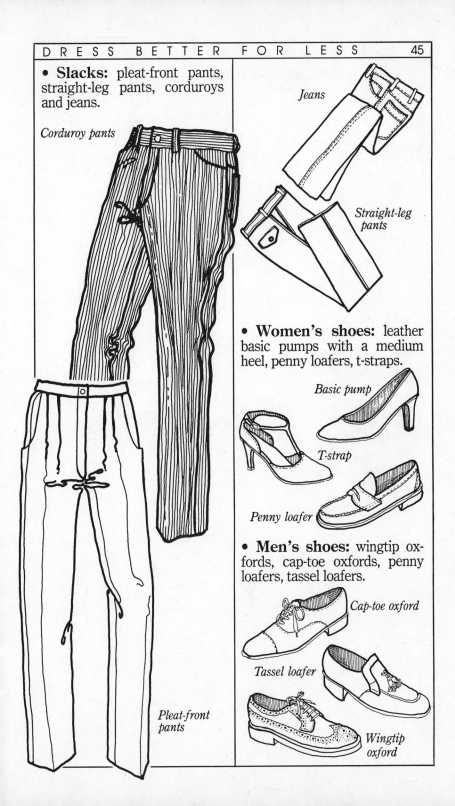

Jeans

Straight-leg pants

- **Women's shoes:** leather basic pumps with a medium heel, penny loafers, t-straps.

Basic pump

T-strap

Penny loafer

- **Men's shoes:** wingtip oxfords, cap-toe oxfords, penny loafers, tassel loafers.

Cap-toe oxford

Tassel loafer

Wingtip oxford

Pleat-front pants

Classic Colors, Patterns and Fabrics

Colors	The classic colors are navy, gray, brown, tan, camel, white, burgundy and heather tones.
Patterns	*Argyle*: A distinctive, diamond-shaped pattern, using two or more colors. *Glen Plaid*: A pattern of small, woven checks alternating with squares of large checks. *Herringbone*: A zigzag-woven pattern, suggesting the skeleton of a fish. Two similar or contrasting colors are used to form the herringbone pattern. *Houndstooth Check*: A small, irregular broken-check pattern. *Tattersall Check*: A pattern of colored lines forming squares of solid background. Also known as window plaid.

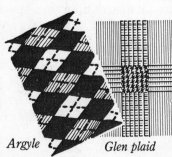 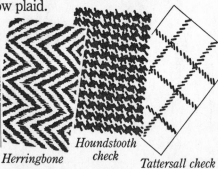

Argyle   *Glen plaid*   *Herringbone*   *Houndstooth check*   *Tattersall check*

Fabrics	*Camel Hair:* A soft, heavy luxury wool, usually in a light tan color. *Cashmere:* A warm, silky wool blend. Very expensive and very luxurious. In coats, it's usually in a light tan color. *Mohair:* A fine wool angora fabric. Usually creates a shaggy look in a sweater. *Shetland Wool:* A fine woven tweed for jackets; a fuzzy knit for sweaters. *Tweeds:* A roughly surfaced, sturdy cloth used most often in men's sportcoats and women's blazers. Tweed is best when manufactured in a 100% wool fabric. Usually two or more colors are woven together. *Harris Tweed* is a quality of wool that is well suited for durable

(continued)

Classics *(continued)*

tweed garments. It is made from 100% pure Scottish wool taken from Harris sheep, which are raised on the Outer Hebrides Islands. The fiber is coarse but strong, and woven only by weavers who are members of the Harris Tweed Association. These tweeds are preferred for their quality of construction, durability and classic designs. They are identified by the Harris Tweed label. Look for these tweeds, especially when you're shopping second-hand sources.

Classic Designers and Manufacturers

Here are some designers who specialize in manufacturing classic fashions (although you may find other styles that are also made by them). Most of these labels are in the expensive price range. Some traditional men's manufacturers are now also making classic clothes for women. These manufacturers' names are starred.

Women's Wear
J.G. Hook
Austin Hill
John Meyer
Harve-Benard
Stanley Blacker
Jaeger
Bogner
Braemar
Gordon's
Jerry Silverman
Evan Picone
Pendelton
Pringle
Alan Paine
Ralph Lauren
Liz Claiborne
Jones of New York
Harris Tweed
Basking Ridge
Schrader Sport
London Fog

Pringle of Scotland
Anne Klein
Howard B. Wolf
Mary McFadden
J.G. Hook

Men's Wear
★Calvin Klein
  Alexander Julian
  Gant
★Barry Bricken
  Corbin
  Country Britches
★Borenstein
★Deansgate
  Chaps
  Bill Blass
  Bert Pulitzer
  Tricot St. Raphael
★Arthur Chaprich
★Thompson
  Woolrich

Evan Picone
Botany 500
Alan Paine
Jaymar
Pendelton
Pringle
Oritsky
Cole-Haan
Braemar
Burberry
San Remo
London Fog
Pierre Cardin
Harris Tweed
★Brooks Brothers

Children's Wear
Florence Eiseman
Fischer Coats
Imp
Ruth of California
London Fog
Lacoste/Izod

Fads and Fashions

Some experts say that in order to save money when you are buying a trendy item, you must buy early. You'll be able to wear it longer and get the most value per wear. This is a good idea, but it's difficult to do if you have trouble spotting a fad that will stick around for a while.

Designer jeans are a good example of this. When they first came out, everyone said they were just a trend. But they have lasted for several years. If you held off buying and were waiting for the lower prices when the rage fizzled, you have probably wasted some good wearing time.

Fashion fads come and go. Some stick around long enough to make it worthwhile to buy into them. Others return years later and make you wish you had kept some of those trendy items.

Take a look at the following chart of clothing fads that will help you reflect back on past trends—and may give you some insight into spotting future ones!

What is a fad?

A fad is a look that has enormous appeal for a short time and then passes. To determine what is just a fad and what will become fashionable requires some canny guesswork.

Some fads remain in style for a long time. This happens when the clothes or accessories are well designed and fit a functional wardrobe need. The key word here is *functional.* When a new clothing item is truly useful, it moves out of the fad category. However, there may follow more trendy offshoots.

An example of this is down-filled coats. They are warm yet lightweight and useful to anyone living in a cold climate. When they first appeared in the marketplace, you could buy only a basic jacket. Today there's a wide variety of styles of down-filled coats, from casual to dressy. Read the following "fad tip-offs" to help avoid buying mistakes.

• **Look for unnecessary details**—fussy styling, extra buttons, pockets, trim. These will quickly date an item.

• **Watch for loud colors:** they become tiresome and are easily spotted as a frequent wardrobe repeater. If you want to brighten your wardrobe, do it with accessories. They won't be as costly or as obvious.

• **Avoid any extreme** in skirt lengths or pant widths. Your clothes will be more comfortable, you'll want to wear them more often and you can make alteration updates.

• **Don't bear down too hard on your teenagers** for buying into fads. The peer influence is important and heavy. If you'll remember back, part of your favorite memories of high school are of the crazy clothes you wore. You may want to encourage them to shop second-hand or at less expensive clothing sources.

Fads or Fashion?

Several of these fads have repeated themselves over the years. Some of us hope that a few of them will never be seen again!

Fads that Have Come and Gone
- Women's padded shoulder suits
- Bobby sox and saddle shoes
- Poodle skirts with crinolines
- Tent dresses
- Pill-box hats
- Pedal pushers
- Mini-skirts
- Maxi-coats
- Tight white vinyl boots
- Stacked platform shoes
- Nehru jackets

Fads that Have Remained Fashionable
- Bikinis
- Jeans
- T-shirts
- Loafers (tassel and penny)
- Short dress boots for men
- Tennis shoes
- Peasant blouses and skirts
- Navy pea coats
- Leather bomber jackets
- Down-filled vests

Peasant blouse

Peasant skirt

Mini-skirt

White vinyl boots

Are All Preppy Clothes Classic?

The current fashion trend toward "preppy" clothes is great news for the shopper who likes the look of traditional classic clothes. It's also a shopping advantage when buying at second-hand sources (where you may find a variety of preppy clothes). Preppy clothing styles are generally conservative; they've been around for a long time, and they're made with fine fabrics and quality construction. However, it's important to remember that not all preppy clothes are necessarily classics. Here's a list of "preppy classics" (clothes that are in traditional styles and make good clothing investments) and of "preppy fads" (clothes that may be in preppy styles but that do not represent the classic look).

Peter Pan-collar blouse

Cardigan sweater

Plaid wool kilt

Tassel loafers

Polo shirt

Khaki hiking shorts

Top-sider shoes

Preppy Classics
- Women's basic pump heels and flats
- Top-sider sailing shoes (not the square toe)
- Peter Pan-collar blouses
- Basic shirtdresses
- Khaki A-line skirts
- Plaid wool kilts
- Leather purses with the coach trademark
- Pearls
- Penny or tassel loafers
- Wingtip shoes for men
- Button-down collar Oxford shirts
- Tweed sportcoats
- Navy flannel blazers with brass buttons
- Lacoste (alligator) sports shirts (other animals are also found on polo shirts—only the "true preppy" insists on alligators)
- Polo shirts
- Tartan plaid wool pants for men
- Khaki, cuffed slacks for men and women
- Wide-wale corduroys and gray flannels for men and women
- Khaki hiking shorts for men and women
- Sweaters for men and women: crew-neck Shetland wool sweaters; Fair Isle cardigans or pullovers; hand-knit Irish fisherman pullovers; V-neck, cable-knit tennis pullovers with stripes around cuffs, waist and V-neck
- Men's cashmere V-neck sweaters
- Trench coats
- Chesterfield coats

Preppy Clothes (*continued*)

Preppy Fads
- Gucci loafers with gold buckles
- Gold snake belts
- Diane Von Furstenberg wrap dresses
- Turtlenecks with small prints (strawberries, hearts, daisies)
- Dayglo-colored, short rubber moccasins
- Painter's pants
- Pappagallo blossom flat shoes in bright pastels
- Bright thong sandals
- Wrap-around, short skirts with polka dots inside and strawberries on the outside
- Alligators on belts, shoes, pants (and on practically anything)

- Corduroy slacks embroidered with spouting whales
- Men's needlepoint monogrammed belts
- Bermuda bag purses (wooden-handled, with changeable cloth covers in bright colors)
- Top-sider shoes, but worn without socks
- Men's boxer shorts, worn ridiculously long
- Cardigan sweaters, buttoned down the back
- Clothes in natural fibers only, giving a wrinkled look to the entire wardrobe
- Preppy "punk" clothes (tightly fitting pedal pushers, mini-skirt length T-shirts and spike heels)

Care Labels

The Federal Trade Commission's regulation for care labeling became effective in 1972. This meant that all garments, including imported clothing, had to be labeled with care instructions. The exceptions are washable items selling for less than $3.00 and leather or suede garments. (Fabric stores must also give care labels with the purchase of material, but sometimes you may have to remind the salesperson.)

The current labeling system has been under criticism since it began.

The four major gripes

• **Drycleaning.** If a garment is labeled as drycleanable, often it is also washable, unless it says "dry clean only" or "do not wash." Manufacturers are only required to recommend *one* method, so most will label conservatively and specify drycleaning when special washing care is also possible.

• **Bleach.** If a label says "Do not bleach," this can also be a conservative recommendation. The manufacturer may be worried that you would use a bleach improperly.

• **Solvents.** Even if you can dryclean, the drycleaner isn't told whether there is a special solvent that should be used. Some would like this question answered on the care label.

• **Temperature.** Similarly, if you can machine wash, what temperature settings are safe?

• **Rule changes.** These care label gripes may be remedied in late 1981 as the Federal Trade Commission proposes some rule changes. In the meantime, use the chart put out by the American Apparel Manufacturers to help read between the lines of care labels.

Consumer Care Guide for Apparel

When Label Reads:	It Means:
Washable Machine washable Machine wash	Wash, bleach, dry and press by any customary method including commercial laundering
Home launder only	Same as above but do not use commercial laundering
No bleach	Do not use bleach
No starch	Do not use starch
Cold wash Cold setting Cold rinse	Use cold water from tap or cold washing machine setting
Warm wash Warm setting Warm rinse	Use warm water—90° to 110° Fahrenheit
Hot wash Hot setting	Use hot water (hot washing machine setting)—130° Fahrenheit or hotter
No spin	Remove wash load before final machine spin cycle
Delicate cycle Gentle cycle	Use appropriate machine setting; otherwise wash by hand

Durable
  press cycle
Permanent
  press cycle
	Use appropriate machine setting; otherwise use medium wash, cold rinse and short spin cycle

Wash separately	Wash alone or with like colors
Hand washable Hand wash	Launder only by hand in lukewarm (hand-comfortable) water. May be bleached. May be drycleaned.
Hand wash only	Same as above, but do not dryclean
Hand wash separately	Hand wash alone or with like colors

(continued)

Consumer Care Guide *(continued)*

When Label Reads:	It Means:
Tumble dry Machine dry	Dry in tumble dryer at specified setting: high, medium, low or no heat
Tumble dry Remove promptly	Same as above, but in absence of cool-down cycle remove at once when tumbling stops
Drip dry Hang dry Line dry	Hang wet and allow to dry with hand-shaping only
No squeeze No wring No twist	Hang dry, drip dry or dry flat only
Dry flat	Lay garment on flat surface
Block to dry	Maintain original size and shape while drying
Cool iron	Set iron at lowest setting
Warm iron	Set iron at medium setting
Hot iron	Set iron at hot setting
No iron No press	Do not iron or press with heat
Steam iron Steam press	Iron or press with steam
Iron damp	Dampen garment before ironing
Dryclean Dryclean only	Garment should be drycleaned only, including self-service

Professionally clean
  only
Commercially clean
  only
	Do not use self-service drycleaning

No dryclean	Use recommended care instructions. No drycleaning materials to be used.

This chart is published by the American Apparel Manufacturers Association and was developed by the Consumer Affairs Committee of the American Apparel Manufacturers Association.

Care Symbols

Imported garments from Canada, Great Britain and Europe use care labels with the instructions in the form of symbols. The five basic symbols in this column are from the International Textile Care Labeling Code. Look at the next column for examples of these symbols as they would actually appear on clothing.

Wash tub
Gives instructions for laundering and washing. A water temperature setting may appear inside this symbol.

Triangle
Gives instructions for bleaching.

Square
Gives instructions for drying.

Circle
Gives instructions for drycleaning. You will want to point out the information on this label to your drycleaner.

Flat iron
Gives instructions for ironing or hand pressing.

Washing instructions

 Wash in lukewarm water.

 Hand wash only.

Bleaching instructions
Use chlorine bleach as directed on container.

Drying instructions
Tumble dry.

Hang to dry.

Dry on flat surface.

Drip dry.

Drycleaning instructions
Use perchlorethylene or petroleum solvent.

Use petroleum solvent only.

Use any solvent.

Ironing instructions
Use cool iron (225° F).

Use warm iron (300° F).

Use hot iron (400° F).

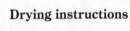

Missing care labels

- **Read** the fiber content label.
- **Determine** if there's a sensitive fiber in the blend (see pages 31–33), such as silk, rayon or wool.
- **Treat** the garment with care for the most sensitive fiber in the blend.

Handle with care

William Seitz of the Neighborhood Cleaners Association in New York suggests that the following fabrics require special handling. They can be a drycleaning risk.

- **Silk** usually drycleans well, but perspiration will rot it. Water, perfume and deodorant will cause color loss. Brightly dyed silks from Hong Kong, Korea or the Philippines may bleed easily. But many of the pale-colored silks are washable.
- **Prints and dyes** may cause trouble. Be careful with any fabric that is top dyed or surface printed. Top dyeing will fade in creases and cracks. A surface print can fade or melt in the drycleaning process. Turn a fabric over to see if color or print is on both sides.
- **Sequins, beads, lamé and glitter** may be only surface coated and may dissolve in normal drycleaning. When the sequins are only glued on the fabric, you have a drycleaning risk. The cleaning method may dissolve the glue.
- **Acrylic knitwear** (Orlon, Acrilan, Creslan) may stretch when hand washed or drycleaned. Gentle-cycle drycleaning is suggested.
- **Suede and leather** must be brought to an expert leather cleaner (see page 134). Bright colors may bleed.

Be a smart drycleaning customer

Clothes with difficult-to-care-for fabrics are often put on sale racks because they are expensive to maintain. You can save time, trouble and money on clothes that are labeled *dryclean only* by being a smart drycleaning customer.

- **Take time to shop around** for an inexpensive drycleaner. Try reading the ads in your local community newspaper; you may find a neighborhood cleaner that charges as much as $1.00 less per item.
- **Consider using the "bulk cleaner" machines** at your local laundromat. This is a good method of "self-cleaning," especially useful for sweaters, solid-color tops and clothes that have been successfully drycleaned in the past. *Don't* try this method on clothes that are labeled "professionally clean only" or "commercially clean only" or those that need careful pressing as well, like suit jackets.
- **Inspect your clothes for spots** before you bring them to the cleaners. Point out any stains. The counter person should mark or make note of stains and discuss any cleaning difficulties with you.

• **Act fast,** and bring stained clothes quickly to the cleaners. Stains do set. Be careful when pressing clothes you've already worn: the heat will set the stain.

• **Talk directly to the drycleaner/spotter** when you are concerned about a fragile fabric. Ask for a fabric test first.

• **Check drycleaned garments immediately,** before you pay or leave the establishment. Look for the removal of stains, shrinkage, stretching or yellowing.

Don't get taken to the cleaners

Even the best of drycleaners can ruin an outfit. But not all garment damage is the fault of the cleaner. If you have a costly outfit that has been ruined and the cleaner pleads innocent, there's a way to get your money back.

• **If your cleaner is a member of the International Fabricare Institute,** he or she can send your garment to the Institute for an analysis. This analysis will determine who is responsible for the damage: the drycleaner or the clothing manufacturer.

• **If the manufacturer is responsible,** you can take the analysis report to the store you bought your outfit from. This report will give you grounds for demanding your money back. It will also give you a leg to stand on in small claims court if the drycleaner or store refuses to pay you.

• **Institute members:** The Better Business Bureau, your local Consumer Protection Agency, your local department store and drycleaner are probably all members of the International Fabricare Institute.

Signs of a quality drycleaner

1. If the pressers do hand finishing.

2. If minor sewing repairs, loose buttons and dangling hems are fixed automatically.

3. If there's no smell of drycleaning fluid in the clothes. This odor can be a sign of an improperly filtered cleaning solvent.

4. If the cleaner will re-press an item at no charge when you are not completely satisfied.

5. If the clothes are bagged properly. There should not be too many clothes in one bag (this causes wrinkling).

6. If your good suit holds its press for several wearings before needing cleaning again.

7. If the drycleaner is a member of the International Fabricare Institute. This will tell you that the drycleaner is well-informed. The Institute keeps its members updated on fabric research and cleaning technology. It also may help you if you have a claim to take up with the drycleaner.

Fabric Stain and Spot Removal

To find the best possible stain chart, I asked household cleaning expert Lois Millner to contribute her stain and spot removal know-how. Lois is an avid second-hand shopper and knows how to deal with stubborn stains. Read her chart and find out how to remove spots from both new and second-hand clothes. This chart will help you determine whether to buy a spotted second-hand garment. If it's a stain that can easily be removed, you will have a good buy. You can bargain with the stain to get the price down and then remove it later. If the stain can't be removed, and you've only paid 50¢ for the item, you've bargained the price down so that you haven't lost that much.

Stain removal tips

• **Supplies.** Try to keep the following supplies on hand: ammonia, bar soap, chlorine bleach, drycleaning fluid, lemon juice, liquid hand dishwashing detergent, rubbing alcohol, turpentine and white vinegar.

• **Fabric.** Success in removing stains depends on the right method of treatment combined with the proper ingredients and the time to let them work properly on the fabric. It's very important to identify the fabric you're treating; look at the care label or hang tag on the garment for this information.

• **Promptness.** Face the stain and work at removing it while the stain is still fresh. If you let the stain set, or if you machine-dry the item before treating it, the stain may be impossible to get out!

• **Pretesting.** Test the stain removal treatment you plan to use on an inconspicuous portion of the item (such as an inside seam or hem) to be sure it will not hurt the garment.

• **Color fastness.** Check the fabric for color fastness before using chlorine bleach on it. Mix 1 tablespoon of bleach with ¼ cup of water; then try a drop of this liquid on an inside seam of the item. If the color doesn't change, you'll be safe in bleaching the garment.

• **Rubbing.** Don't rub or dab heavily at the problem area. Rubbing causes fuzziness, which in turn attracts more surface soil.

Unknown stains

Don't be afraid to treat uncommon or unknown stains that are not listed in the stain chart!

• **If the stains are greasy** and the fabric is washable, sponge with detergent, let stand for a few minutes and wash; repeat if necessary.

• **If the stains are non-greasy** and the fabric is washable, soak it in cool water for at least 30 minutes, rub in some detergent and rinse thoroughly; bleach with a mild solution if necessary.

• **If the fabric is nonwashable,** sponge it with detergent and follow this with a small application of rubbing alcohol to remove the detergent. Good luck!

Stains in antique clothes

Do use caution when cleaning antique or vintage clothes, as the stains may have been set in for decades!

• **If you have a garment made of unusual fabric** (such as lamé, silk/pongee or fake fur), talk to an antique or vintage clothing store owner about the stain and ask for recommendations on how to deal with it.

• **If the stain or fabric seems tricky to handle,** ask the store owner which professional cleaner he or she uses. You may find that the store owner has a reliable source to recommend—or the owner may give you some special tips you've never heard of!

Stain Removal Chart

Stain	How to Remove
Adhesive tape, chewing gum	First rub with ice; then scrape off. Lightly sponge the area with drycleaning fluid, rinse and wash.
Alcoholic beverages	Soak in cool water. Then sponge with white vinegar, rinse well and wash.
Ballpoint pen ink	Sponge lightly with rubbing alcohol. Wash, using chlorine bleach.*
Blood	Soak in cool water for at least 45 minutes. Rub with bar soap and then wash. If stain persists, soak in a solution of 2 tablespoons of ammonia to 1 gallon of cold water, and wash, using chlorine bleach.
Catsup, tomato sauce, baby formula	Soak in warm water with liquid dishwashing detergent and a drop of ammonia. Rinse and wash.
Chocolate, cocoa, coffee, egg, gravy, meat juice, tea	Run cool water over the stained area, rub with liquid detergent and soak. If stain persists, sponge with drycleaning fluid, rinse and wash.

(continued)

Stain Chart *(continued)*

Stain	How to Remove
Grass	Sponge with liquid detergent and rinse. If stain persists, apply rubbing alcohol, rinse and wash.
Grease, ice cream, mayonnaise, milk, oil, tar	Apply liquid detergent to the stain, let stand, rinse and wash. If stain persists, sponge with drycleaning fluid, rinse and wash.
Lipstick, liquid make-up, mascara	Soak in drycleaning fluid and let dry. Rinse and then wash.
Mustard	Rub with liquid detergent, rinse and wash. If stain persists, wash with chlorine bleach.
Paint, varnish	Wash out stain before paint or varnish dries on. Soak in turpentine (unless the fabric is made of acetate). Rinse and wash, using extra detergent.
Perspiration	Rub with liquid detergent, rinse and wash. If stain persists, apply ammonia or white vinegar, rinse and wash.
Rust	Rub with lemon juice, dry and wash.
Urine	Soak in cool water, apply liquid detergent, rinse and wash. If stain persists, sponge with white vinegar, rinse and wash.
Vomit	Soak in solution of 1 cup of salt to 1 gallon of cool water, rinse and wash. If stain persists, apply a few drops of ammonia, rinse and wash.
Yellowing	Soak in solution of ½ cup of chlorine bleach and 1 tablespoon of white vinegar to 1 gallon of warm water. Rinse thoroughly and wash. If stain persists, repeat treatment and dry in the sunshine.

*Don't use chlorine bleach on *any* stain unless you have tested the fabric for color fastness first (see page 57).

Shop Around for Prices

A shopkeeper in New York's oldest garment district on Orchard Street once told me, "In this town you can buy anything and not pay the full retail price." That's true almost anywhere, *if* you shop around for the best prices. When you pay the full retail price for new clothes, you are paying a 100% mark-up—who needs it?

Buy it right

• **Look for sales.** Read newspaper ads; check sale flyers in your mail; get on a catalog mailing list.

• **Look for bargain racks** or tables whenever you are in a store. Ask salesclerks if there are any special sales that day.

• **Look for seasonal sales** (see page 12). You can save money when you buy early on in the sale, and you'll find a better selection of items then.

Buy it second-hand

To determine a good second-hand price (see page 61), you must first have the answer to these questions:

• What's the new price?

• Is this an item I could find at close to the second-hand price, when it goes on sale, or maybe at a discount store?

Using your answers as a price guide, consider this:

• **If the new price is $50.00 and the second-hand price is $30.00,** the sale price new will probably be one-third off, or $35.00. The lower price is not enough of a price reduction to warrant a search for the same item, second-hand.

• **If the new price is $75.00 and the second-hand price is $40.00,** the sale price will be one-third off, or $52.50. If the condition of the second-hand garment is *near new*, buy the second-hand item.

To Sew or Buy?

If you sew, you're very fortunate because you will save lots of money on your wardrobe. There are times, however, when your time and effort are worth more to you than the money you can save. There will be other times when the cost of fabric, plus the cost of your energy, will be much more than a sale price on a garment. Maybe an article of clothing will take more sewing skills than you possess. Or perhaps you have a problem with fitting whenever you try to make yourself a pair of slacks. These are all good reasons to buy rather than sew.

Saving money if you sew

• **Look for fabrics at bargain sources:** garage sales, thrift stores, discount fabric stores and factory outlet stores.

Price Chart	Retail: Better Quality	Retail: Average Quality	Catalog Sales	Outlet Store	Resale Shop	Men's Designer Discount	Women's Designer Discount	Goodwill	Thrift	Children's Consignment
Man's suit	$150–300	$100–130	$95–130	$60–90	$20–75	$155		$5–20	$10–25	
Woman's suit	$130–150	$32–55	$30–55	$19–30	$4–70		$50–130	$5–10	$10–15	
Man's cloth coat	$125	$80	$79	$50–75	$4–40	$125		$4–15	$10–20	
Woman's coat	$150–190	$95	$90	$60–80	$4–60		$60–up	$4–15	$5–15	
Man's long-sleeved shirt	$15–35	$10–15	$10–15	$8–12	$2–8	$20		$2	$2–4	
Woman's long-sleeved blouse	$30	$15–20	$12–20	$8–12	$2–10		$10–up	$2	$2	
Man's slacks	$25	$19	$18	$12	$4–10	$25		$3	$3–10	
Woman's slacks	$55	$16	$14	$10	$4–15		$10–70	$3	$3–7	
Dress	$40–150	$30	$29	$16–25	$4–60		$13–50	$5–10	$3–10	
Skirt	$55	$20	$16	$12	$5–25		$13–50	$4–7	$2–5	
Child's dressy outfit	$50	$30	$25	$18				$2	$4	$4–10
Child's play outfit	$30	$12	$11	$8				$2	$3	$2–8
Infant's snowsuit	$40	$20	$24	$17				$4	$5	$6
Child's snowmobile suit	$60	$21	$21	$18				$5	$5	$8

• **Avoid costly fabrics** such as velvet or ultra-suede. This is especially important when you are attempting a difficult pattern for the first time.

• **Look for kits that will help you make outdoor clothing** (not to mention sleeping bags and other gear). Most people who know how to run a sewing machine can assemble them, and the savings can be great—especially when you're outfitting a family. (See page 153 for sources.)

Saving money if you don't sew

Consider custom sewing. If you're after classic investment clothing, need unique designs, or are hard to fit, comparison shop between stores and tailors or seamstresses. Sometimes the total cost—fabric, pattern and labor—comes out lower if you have things custom-made. A typical cost for a custom-made men's three-piece suit (done in good quality wool) is $300.00. A similar suit for women, but as a two-piece outfit, would cost $210.00. (These costs reflect labor and material.)

• **Watch for ads for visiting tailors** who set up shop in hotel suites and take orders and measurements for custom work. If you know your prices, you can occasionally find good (though by no means inexpensive) prices on well-done custom work. Be sure to find out if the tailor deals directly with the manufacturer; some tailors have no direct contact with the source, and this can result in higher prices and inferior workmanship.

When to Sew and When to Buy

Here's a chart that will help you choose the quickest and easiest route when determining whether to sew or buy.

Sew	Sew or Buy	Buy
T-shirts	Blouses	Men's suits
Shorts	Slacks	Men's sportcoats
Jogging suits	Culottes	Blazers
Lingerie (pajamas,	Pleated skirts	Coats
underwear,	Easy blazers**	Children's winter
nightgowns)*		outerwear
Plain dresses		Jeans
Skirts (no pleats)		Furs
Jumpers		

*It's very inexpensive to make lingerie, but you should take a lingerie class and learn the best way to sew with the fabric. You'll find it well worth your time.

**To choose an easy blazer pattern, look for a collar designed to be part of the facing, one sleeve pattern piece, two fronts and one back. A more difficult blazer pattern will have additional pattern pieces.

Bargain Shopping Checklist

Before you buy, answer these questions and see if you're really getting a bargain.

☐ Are you getting the best quality workmanship? Be sure you've checked seams, stitches, fabric and design.

☐ Is the fabric durable, good-looking and one that won't be too expensive to maintain? If the fabric requires drycleaning, is it one that will not be a cleaning risk?

☐ Is the garment a classic design, one that you will wear for many seasons? Or if it's a trendy item, are you buying at the beginning, middle or end of the trend?

☐ Does the garment fit properly and enhance your best features? Is the garment going to require expensive alterations?

☐ Is the price of the garment reasonable, high or a real steal for what you're purchasing? Would you be better off sewing the item yourself?

Hassle-Free Guide for Shoppers

1. Shop when stores are least crowded to save time and energy. Salespeople are always more helpful at these times. Best days: Monday, Tuesday and Friday. Best hours: mornings before 11:30 a.m.; mid-afternoons between 2:30 and 4:00 p.m.; evenings at dinner time, 6:00 to 7:00 p.m.

2. Shop when the weather is bad. You may be the only hardy shopper in the store!

3. Educate yourself to the store's layout. If you're not in familiar territory, use the store's information service (if there is one). It's often quicker than asking a salesperson.

4. Come prepared when you attend a sale. The day before, study store ads and sale flyers. List the sale items you want, their prices and the departments where they'll be. Doing this saves you time and helps prevent impulse buying.

5. Charge or use cash when you're in a hurry. Getting a check approved can slow you down.

6. Bring young children (and for some, husbands) shopping only on short trips, for obvious reasons.

Finding New Clothes For Less

In the movie *Manhattan*, Woody Allen remarks, "In my family, the biggest sin was to buy retail." This statement rang in my ears long after I made one of my worst buying mistakes.

I was leaving for New York and on an impulse, I decided I needed a blazer for the trip. I had an appointment downtown and twenty minutes to kill, so I dashed into a ritzy women's store and bought a white blazer for $150.00. This was in the middle of October.

Two weeks later I went to Loehmann's, a designer discount store, with a friend. There I saw a white blazer marked down to $29.99. It was designed a little differently than mine but was definitely a style I would have been happy with—and it looked great on me! I never could wear my own $150.00 white blazer again without feeling foolish and frivolous. Six credit card payments later, I vowed never to buy another new item that wasn't discounted from its full price.

That impulsive purchase was just part of my mistake. I realized later that my timing had been terrible. Since I was buying in the middle of October, I could have found a great selection in the discount stores then. And if only I had waited three more weeks, the blazer I bought would have been put on sale in the fancy store as well.

The point is this: to be a bargain shopper you must have patience. Not a lot, but enough to sustain you until your favorite discount store gets its mid-season shipment. Or you can haunt the racks of your favorite retail store and wait like a vulture, ready to swoop when the items you need go on sale.

This chapter will help you be a skilled bargain hunter. It presents the specific buying know-how you need to shop all kinds of discounted sources of new clothes, from retail clearance sales to factory outlets. As you read, you'll find a description of each type of source and how to find such sources in your area. You'll learn the pros and cons of shopping at each source, what clothes you can expect to find there, what the source's policies are and how much money you should save by shopping there. Finally, you'll discover special shopping tips that will make bargain hunting easier for you.

Take the bargain hunter's personality test and see if you pass. If you do, you'll save money, feel less guilty about your purchases and avoid costly buying mistakes. Let this chapter teach you to be a successful bargain shopper.

Bargain Hunter's Personality Test

Ask yourself these questions to see if you have a bargain hunter's personality.

1. Can you eavesdrop on "good sale" conversations at the bus stop—or better yet, at an adjacent table while you're dining by candlelight with a special friend? ☐ Yes ☐ No

2. Can you find a heightened sense of drama and excitement while pressed back-to-back with other bargain hunters, waiting for a sale to start?
☐ Yes ☐ No

3. Can you forget all about your tennis date when a friend calls to report a new shipment of Anne Klein blazers at your favorite discount store?
☐ Yes ☐ No

4. Do you have the stamina required to skim through rows of clothes racks, dig through stacks of clothes and carry armloads of "possible finds" to the dressing room? (All of this activity may be enough exercise to substitute for your body-building or slimnastics class!) ☐ Yes ☐ No

5. Can you try on your bargain selections without concern for personal modesty, in a community dressing room—or worse yet, the middle of a store? ☐ Yes ☐ No

6. Can you show your assertiveness and get your way, even when you are about to be cut off just as you're making a grab at a discount rack?
☐ Yes ☐ No

7. Does part of your thrill in finding a good buy come later, when you retell your "great deal" story to friends?
☐ Yes ☐ No

8. When you walk into a department store, do you scoff at the undiscounted retail prices and walk out, knowing you can find the same outfits for much less? ☐ Yes ☐ No

Scoring:

0 yes answers: You'd better change your attitude if you're after bargains—or else come into a fortune!

0–2 yes answers: You've got potential, but you need to get bolder and try some of the tips you'll read in this book.

3–4 yes answers: You've got lots of potential, but you definitely need some practice to really cut clothes costs.

5–6 yes answers: You're probably already a good bargain hunter. The bargain sources and tips for shopping there will extend and improve on your ability.

7–8 yes answers: You're really able to dress better for less—congratulations!

Bargain Shopping Vocabulary

First quality	Merchandise that's in perfect condition. By law, if an item is an irregular or a second (see page 15), it must be so marked.
Odd-lots, mill-ends, bolt-ends, remnants, piece goods	Items that result when a small amount of merchandise or material is left unsold, after retailers have ordered. Factory outlets will often sell this leftover merchandise. It is usually first quality.
Overstocks, overruns, over-cuts, over-orders	Merchandise that was manufactured over the amount of orders sold to the retailer. This merchandise is sold to discounters or through the factory's outlet store. It is also first-quality merchandise.
Discontinued or cancelled goods	Merchandise that's no longer being produced by the manufacturer. These goods can be first-quality items, seconds or irregulars.
Returns	Merchandise that's refused by the retailer, often due to late delivery.
Samples	Merchandise that the manufacturer or the manufacturer's representative (rep or salesman) has made up to show to buyers and other retail clients before they order. It may also be used for models or displays. This merchandise often ends up being sold in sample shops or at the salesman's own garage sale (see page 83.)
Jobber	A middleman who buys large amounts of merchandise from a manufacturer and then sells to store owners. Any time a jobber is involved, the merchandise cannot be discounted for as much as it can when bought directly by a discount store. Sometimes jobbers sell in their own stores and call the stores "outlets," but these are not true factory outlet stores. You will save money at a jobber's outlet store, but you'll save more when you go directly to a real factory outlet.
Job Lot	Merchandise of all types brought together and sold in one quantity by a jobber.

Retail Department Stores

Some of my best childhood memories are of shopping for clothes with my grandmother. She loved to hit the various sales at her favorite department store. We would take the streetcar downtown early in the morning and wait in a crowd of women for the store to open.

I followed in amazement as my very reserved grandmother raced into the store as soon as the doors opened and headed for the bargain tables. There she elbowed out the other women, grabbed her sale prizes, and ran with her winnings to the cash register. When finished, she would announce that as a reward for saving so much money we would lunch downtown and take a cab home. Today, I credit my grandmother for introducing me to the sport of shopping.

Retail department stores such as grandmother's offer excellent buys at their various sales, especially when the economy is down. In bad times, the selection of sale merchandise will be good and markdowns will start early in the season. The slowest months for retail stores are January, February and March, so shop the sales during these times. Watch for clearances and special sales at other times, too. Take advantage of a tight economy: you'll be money ahead if you do.

Background

Department stores sell clothes, grouped by categories like women's, boys' and other specialized subdivisions, but they also sell other goods. They include Sears, Penney's and Ward's plus other chains and individual stores. They do *not* call themselves "discount" stores. Merchandise is generally sold at full retail (list) prices at the beginning of the time it is in season, but gets reduced throughout the season and at clearances and other special sales. (See page 12 for the annual sales calendar.)

- **How to find:** look in the yellow pages (*Department Stores*), check local papers for ads (especially on Wednesday and Sunday) and ask for guidebooks to local stores at libraries and bookstores.

Department Store Policies

Savings ....15–50% off list (10–25% off list at Sears, Penney's and Ward's)

Credit ....store charges, bank credit cards, checks with ID, cash

Returns ....yes, except when marked "all sales final"

Lay-by.................varies—ask

Services ....alterations, deliveries, phone and mail orders, shoe and jewelry repair, personal shopping services (varies with the store)

Announcements ....sale flyers, radio and TV ads

Rainchecks ......usually—ask

Tactics for Shopping Department Stores

1. Familiarize yourself with the store's best merchandise. Then when it's advertised at sale price you'll know you're getting a good deal.

2. If you're interested in buying high-fashion clothes (designer labels and imported garments), hold off your buying for a few weeks each season and save at least 15% on the first reduction. As the season wears on, the clothes will be marked down even more.

3. Look first for a sale rack whenever you shop. Often a department has a rack tucked away from the main traffic area, even when a major sale is not being held.

4. If you frequently shop a particular store, familiarize yourself with their special store promotion times. The weeks before and after Christmas, the end of each month and special annual sales are worth planning around. (See page 12.)

5. Be wary of "special purchase sales" (or "special sales"). If you see that language, the items may be brought in just for the sale. Other tip-offs: racks full of identical items and price tags with only one clean price showing. Ask clerks why the sale is being held.

6. Take a chance at a sneak preview of a sale. I try to shop the night before a sale starts, when the salespeople are setting out the merchandise for the next day. As soon as the sale items are put on the racks you can buy. Not all of the merchandise will be put out, but you'll get first choice on some of the items. Otherwise, aim for the first day of a sale for the best selections.

7. Check sale items carefully for damage. If a garment is marked "as is," and the damage is minor, don't automatically discard the item. You may still be getting a bargain even with the cost of repair. Damaged goods *not* marked "as is" may be worth bargaining on.

Common clothing finds

In addition to various clothing departments, there may be a "haute couture" section. Major department stores (except Sears, Penney's and Ward's) sell designer clothing and accessories for men, women and children.

• **Look for bargain basements,** especially in downtown department stores.

• **Look for markdowns** as each season progresses.

• **Look for a bargain room or rack** where regular merchandise is sold at cut prices.

Advantages

• **Sales at department stores** can save money—and the variety is generally very good.

• **Store charge accounts** can help spread your expenses out.

• **Central locations and time-saving services** (phone and mail orders, deliveries, wardrobe planning) and one-stop shopping make department stores good bets for efficient shopping.

Disadvantages

• **If you lean toward impulse buying,** a large department store can easily put you into "credit debt" with its vast selections.

• **If you live for right now** and can't think Christmas during July's heat (and sales), you'll have trouble following the retail sale calendar. You are better off buying discount or second-hand clothes in season.

Bargain Basements

Suburban shopping malls, because they frequently don't even have basements, have reduced some of the interest in bargain basement shopping. Yet today, bargain basements are being rediscovered as smart shoppers try to cut costs. Read the following tips and get into the sport of spotting a good deal when you head for the basements.

Background

Bargain basements are located on the bottom floor of large retail department stores. Expect to find them in downtown department stores rather than suburban shopping malls. They bridge the gap between a retail store and a discount chain store (see page 70). Merchandise is, on the whole, priced lower than in the rest of the store, though you may find a few relatively expensive name brands included in the stock.

• **How to find:** look in the yellow pages *(Department Stores)* and call the major stores to ask if they have bargain basements, budget sections or budget departments. Check the papers too. If a store has a bargain area, you will see it mentioned in its ads.

Bargain Basement Policies

Savings ....can't say— quality is lower than it is upstairs

Other policies................see Department Store Policies (page 67)

Common clothing finds

• **Good deals on wardrobe basics:** underwear, children's clothes; men's, women's and teens' blouses, shirts and sweaters; accessories.

Advantages

• **You can shop a less expensive source** but have access to the same services and wide variety of goods you expect upstairs.

Disadvantages

• **Lower quality and fewer classic lines**—not an ideal source for better-quality items that will last.

Tactics for Shopping Bargain Basements

1. If you know what you need to buy, check out the store's bargain basement first. However, you should then compare goods with merchandise upstairs in order to get the best value. If a better-quality item is only a few dollars more, go for the quality.

2. Check garment construction carefully (see pages 27–30). Then you can choose the best quality item in a given price range.

3. Shop for items that you don't expect long life from: trendy clothing, children's underwear, lingerie, items you only wear occasionally. Teenagers' needs are well met in bargain basements. Consider the value per wear (see page 10).

Discount Chain Stores

Discount chains can inexpensively fill in some missing pieces in your wardrobe. Here are some tips to help you select the best for less when you shop them.

Background

Discount chains are stores such as K-Mart, Walmart, Venture, Woolworth's or Woolco, Target and Fed-Mart. These are stores where you push a cart around and help yourself to all sorts of merchandise, clothing among others. The clothes are all mass-produced items—not name-brand labels or high quality. Discount chains also buy odd lots and don't always offer a full range of sizes and colors for some items, but the prices are lower than those at a retail department store.

• **How to find:** look in the yellow pages (*Department Stores*), but watch for the word *discount* as part of the store's name; also watch for newspaper, radio or TV ads.

Common clothing finds

• **All types of clothes:** for men, women, teenagers and children—from suits to outerwear. Shop discount chains for the same items you look for in bargain basements (items you won't wear often, trendy accessories to update outfits, children's "disposable" items). Expect lots of synthetic fabrics and trendy colors and fewer classic fibers and looks.

• **Shoes:** for the whole family, but not made of fine leather. Look for shoes for fast-growing children, but fit them very carefully.

Discount Chain Policies

Savings ....can't say— quality is lower than at retail department stores
Credit ....bank credit cards, checks with ID, cash
Returns ....yes, except some sale items
Lay-bys ....usually not
Rainchecks...ask about them

Tactics for Shopping Discount Chain Stores

1. Learn how to recognize quality and know when it's not necessary to buy the most expensive items.

2. Watch for advertised sales on necessary household items and clothing. Shop those sales and plan to include the household items along with the clothes to save on both time and money.

3. Read labels! Check out the fabric content and select natural fabrics when they are available. I found a 100% pure wool tweed blazer for $29.99, fully lined and well constructed. I had seen it at Sears the season before for $49.99, and the fabric was also being used by better manufacturers for blazers that were styled differently. This blazer featured notched lapels that would remain in style for some time, so I bought it. The point: when you can spot quality fabrics, construction and styling, you can ferret out the better merchandise and save money at discount chain stores.

4. While you shop, listen for intercom specials. Particular items will be specially priced for short times. If you need something that's announced, head for it quickly. Grab the merchandise; sort and select later.

5. Before you head to the check-out lines, sort through your cart. Determine if you really love all the items you've piled in and then decide which ones to buy.

Advantages

• **If you have time to shop carefully,** a discount chain can offer good buys on standard items, especially for children's and teenagers' clothes.

Disadvantages

• **If you like personal service,** you won't find it at a discount chain store.

• **If you're short on time,** the money you save may not be worth your effort.

Catalog Outlet Stores

A friend's husband claims he is going to build his next house near a Penney's outlet store. Marge shops so frequently at one of Penney's catalog outlet stores and has such good luck clothing their three children with the merchandise she finds that he figures she may as well save gas "commuting."

These stores can be hit-or-miss shopping. It takes time to shop them well, but the savings are big if you do. And if you're a veteran bargain hunter like Marge, you will enjoy the challenge that goes with the search. If you're a novice, you'll want to read the following tips first and then decide whether to give catalog outlets a try.

Background

Catalog outlets are clearance centers for stores like Sears, Penney's and Ward's—stores that generally sell catalog merchandise. All the overstocks, returns and damaged goods from each store's catalog department filter into the outlet. This merchandise is then sold for less than you would pay if you ordered it from the store's catalog department. Some outlets also stock merchandise from their other retail store departments.

• **How to find one:** phone a large department store in your area. Ask if it has a catalog department, and if so, whether there is a clearance outlet for their catalog overstocks. Also check white-page listings under department store names for outlet branches, and scan ads in your newspaper.

Catalog Outlet Policies

Savings...................25–50% off catalog list, and 50–70% off catalog list at clearances
Credit........store credit cards, checks with ID, cash
Returns...........................yes
Lay-bys.........ask about them
Clearances...........same time as catalog sales, but they last longer
Pricing.................tags should show catalog price and discount price—ask for a catalog when in doubt
Damage.................items will be marked—check to see if they're wearable
Stock.....................25–50% of stock arrives when catalog store's does; the rest arrives in spurts thereafter
Best hours...........weekdays, during the day

Common clothing finds

• **Look for clothes for the whole family.** Brand names will probably be the store's own label. Your best bet is clothing basics: underwear, streetwear, jeans, durable work clothes. The quality of these clothes is better than you would find at a discount chain, yet you'll pay less for them.

• **Sizes and selection vary a lot.** Since this merchandise is made up of overstocks, you may see a whole rack of size 5 women's slacks, for instance.

Advantages

• **If you need children's clothes,** a catalog outlet store is a good first stop. The more kids you are buying for, the better your luck will be, since the stock varies unpredictably. Still, the savings on children's clothes may be well worth the shopping time.

• **If you're not after a specific item,** you'll find good deals on clothes for men and women. Look for the clothing basics (underwear and so on) and sportswear.

• **If you want to save time,** combine your clothes shopping with buying items for the house at catalog outlets. You can pick up some good furniture bargains.

Disadvantages

• **If you have limited shopping time,** or want specific items, the unpredictable stock will frustrate you.

Tactics for Shopping Outlet Stores

1. Locate the outlet store ad in your newspaper, and check it weekly to see what items are currently in stock.

2. Phone ahead if you're looking for specific items.

3. Allow yourself enough time to shop. Two hours is a good amount of time, especially if you're really going to comb the store.

4. Ask if the store has an "as is" or damaged section... that's where the biggest savings will be.

5. Ask a salesclerk for a tape measure and the catalog's size chart page if you are unsure about a size. Carry a list of the family's sizes (in inches) with you to save time and guesswork.

6. If only part of an outfit is available at the outlet, check the catalog. You may still be able to complete the outfit by ordering what's missing from the catalog department.

7. Be sure to check the merchandise carefully before you buy. Some items will be shopworn.

8. To bargain, ask to speak to the manager. Bargaining is minimal, but if an item is flawed and not marked "damaged," the price should come down.

9. Shop for back-to-school clothes in August. The selection will be small, but you will get first choice then. If you can combine shopping the outlet with your catalog orders, you can take advantage of the savings at the outlet *and* the back-to-school sale prices that most catalogs offer in August.

Designer Discount Stores

Loyal designer discount store customers are men and women who know quality, style and designer names. They're an educated group who want the best —at a discounted price. Among them you'll find celebrities (Lauren Bacall shopped at one of the oldest designer discount stores in the country, as she proudly mentions in her autobiography), professionals, young people on limited budgets and even the very wealthy.

These designer discount stores have been around for years. The key difference today is the clothing manufacturer's need for the discounter. In the past, clothes were designed for two main seasons—spring and fall. Now, they are being designed for five: fall, cruise, holiday, spring and summer seasons. Overruns abound, and this is where the designer discounters come in, cash in hand, ready to bail out the manufacturers.

There are times when manufacturers even gear their production to accommodate discounters. This trend in retailing means that there is more high-quality discounted clothing available now than ever before. You can cash in on this trend and buy quality constructed clothes fashioned by top designers at great savings.

In this section I will be directing my shopping tips at high-volume designer discount stores, such as Loehmann's and Marshall's, across the country. The discount outlet section (see page 76) relates directly to the smaller designer discount and outlet stores.

Background

Designer discount stores vary in size and decor—they range from supermarket-like barns to smaller, more elegant surroundings. Most stores are located away from major shopping areas (downtown and large suburban malls). This is to protect manufacturers' arrangements with retailers selling the same merchandise at a higher cost.

Designer discount stores and outlet stores buy manufacturers' overruns, irregulars, discontinued styles and retailers' overstock. The high-volume discounters even have extra merchandise made for them.

Marshall's and Loehmann's are two large designer discount stores that purchase in volume, directly from the manufacturer, so there's no middleman. Some smaller outlets have a central purchasing office to get around the middleman too. These stores pass on even better savings than other outlets that do rely on a middleman to do their buying. This is important to know because you may find designer discount stores that do not offer such substantial discounts. You must comparison shop among discounters to get the best price.

• **How to find one:** look in the source directory of this book (see page 159) for the names of stores located near you. Then check your phone book's white pages under those names. Also, look for newspaper ads for stores like Loehmann's and Marshall's and listen for television and radio ads. Ask friends and neighbors if they have ever shopped at a designer discount store. The best advertising for this type of store is done by word of mouth.

Designer Discount Policies

Savings..........20–70% off list
Credit.................bank credit cards (at some), checks with ID, cash
Returns......................varies
Competition...............some won't be undersold, so comparison shop
Labels.....................some cut out labels to protect regular retailers who sell at list (see page 40 for ways to learn who designed the clothes; also check the lining for woven-in names and initials in men's clothes)
Seasons...............April–May for spring; August–October for fall; November–December for holiday and cruise
Stock.................should come in weekly—ask
Checking...................parcels and coats may be kept aside
Protecting selections........ hang clothes you want (or want to try on later) on racks outside dressing rooms. Tie them together—use the "Loehmann's knot" (sleeves tied around the group of clothes)—to signal your interest

Tactics for Shopping Designer Discount Stores

1. If you can shop the early morning hours or during dinner time, you may save yourself time and energy. Weekends, lunch hours and some evenings are crowded with shoppers during the peak discount seasons.

2. If you feel too modest to undress in the company of many other people in the dressing room, it helps to wear a leotard under your clothes. You'll be covered, yet you can still check for a proper fit.

3. Sharpen your eye to current clothing styles and prices before you go to a designer discount store. Many discounters buy discontinued styles—and last year's hot item is not what you're looking for.

4. Prices at a designer discount store may seem high if you're not up on the current retail prices of designer and high-quality clothes. For example, a Halston 100% silk blouse may be discounted from $125.00 to $60.00. If these prices overwhelm you and your budget, consider second-hand sources for designer and high-quality items.

5. Look for classic clothes and check for signs of quality construction and fabric. Bring along this book and use the list of designers who make quality classic clothes (see page 47) and the bargain hunter's shopping guide to pick high-performance items.

6. This is the place to make major wardrobe purchases, so bring a list of your wardrobe needs (see page 7).

7. Bring along a friend whose judgment you trust about what looks good on you. Be sure it's a friend who doesn't wear the same size!

8. Check the condition of all merchandise carefully. If an item is marked *irregular*, don't automatically shy away: find out why. But if the flaw won't interfere with the style or performance of the garment, buy it if the savings are great.

9. Take a chance and save: if you find an outfit you don't need immediately, wait before buying. It may be marked down the following week.

10. Discounters may only cut accessory (purses, belts and so on) prices by 15% to 20%. You can save more money on these items at second-hand stores and at some retail clearance sales.

Common clothing finds

• **Look at Marshall's** for men's, women's (including larger sizes), juniors', children's and infants' clothing. You'll also find other types of merchandise, including household items. Marshall's has first-quality merchandise along with some irregulars.

• **Look at Loehmann's** for women's wear. You'll find a wide range of name-brand and designer clothing and accessories. Loehmann's has an area called "The Back Room" where you'll find better designer clothes. All the merchandise is first quality—no irregulars.

Advantages

• **If you know your stuff**—current fashion, reputable designers' names, quality garment construction and fit—you're a natural for designer discount stores. Just beware of lesser-quality items that will be mixed in with the fine ones.

• **If you want to project an executive look,** a designer discount store will help you fit the image and save you money. A man's suit can be discounted at least $100.00 at a store of this type.

Disadvantages

• **If you have a specific outfit in mind,** you may not find it. Think instead in terms of the type of wardrobe staple (suit, sportcoat, blazer, skirt) you need and what color will work best, rather than the exact style or pattern.

• **If you value certain services and features** (shopping by phone, delivery, uncrowded or even private dressing rooms), these sources are not for you. However, the shopping conditions are not that inconvenient for most shoppers who value the savings.

• **If you only shop infrequently,** you won't always find what you need.

• **If your will-power is low,** you may feel your buying resistance crumble when faced with a great selection of clothes, all at discounted prices.

Discount Outlet Stores

Discount outlet stores are cropping up in small shopping centers across the country. These outlets are not to be confused with factory warehouse outlets (see page 78), which are directly owned by an individual manufacturer. This section will help you understand the difference between these stores and help you choose the discount outlet that will give you a good price on quality items.

Background

A discount outlet store sells various manufacturers' overruns, discontinued styles, samples and some irregulars at discounted prices.

Ownership and buying patterns vary. Some outlets are owned as franchises, and they pay a large central buying office in New York a percentage of their income for this service. Sometimes several outlets are owned by one person. This person purchases from various manufacturers and provides the stock for all the outlets. Some large chain stores have also opened their own outlets. These outlets stock manufacturers' overruns and the chain store's overstocks. Finally, some individual outlets are privately owned. The store owner buys from a jobber (see page 66), who in turn buys from the manufacturers.

The longer the chain of people involved in buying from the

manufacturer, the less you will save on clothes. Before you shop a discount outlet, ask what the discount is—if it's only 20% for the majority of the merchandise, shop elsewhere for better bargains.

• **How to find one:** check the source directory in this book (see page 159) for outlets near you. Take a look at the list of buying-guide books (see page 154); these can also aid you in finding an outlet store. And look in the yellow pages (*Men's Clothing and Furnishings, Women's Apparel* and *Children's and Infants' Wear*).

• **Check libraries** (see page 154) for local guide books and skim newspaper ads. Outlets will advertise but they don't usually tell you what brand names they offer.

• **If you live in a major city** with a garment district, scout it for outlets.

• **Here are some examples** of outlets around the country that offer good discounts: Sym's men's store and The Best Things women's outlet in New York; J. Brannam family apparel outlets in Dallas and Oklahoma; Kids' Mart in California; C & R Clothiers for men, across the country; and Hit or Miss women's outlets, across the country.

Common clothing finds

• **Although there are all-purpose outlets, most specialize in their mer-**

Discount Outlet Policies

Savings...........20-60% off list
Credit ....varies; call ahead
Returns ....usually none
Lay-bys ....none
Services ....alterations on men's clothes—check the charge against what an outside tailor charges
Seasons ....April–May for spring; August–October for fall; November–December for holiday and cruise
Labels ....may be removed (see page 40)
Markdowns ....ask when they will be (towards the end of seasons); shop early when they happen
Irregulars ....should be marked; should be at greatest discount

chandise. You'll find men's, women's and children's outlets. Some are even more specialized, with only maternity or large-size clothing. Expect name-brand items.

Advantages

• **If you need to stretch your clothing dollar,** you can get brand-name and designer clothing right in the season you want to wear your clothes, without waiting for markdowns at a retail store.

• **If you need a conservative men's suit for work,** a men's outlet store will save you money and time. Most of them are easy to shop and well stocked, especially if you're shopping with the idea that a navy, gray or brown suit will work for you.

• **If you need to buy clothes for children from two to twelve years old,** look for a children's outlet. Be sure to shop at the beginning of the season.

Disadvantages

• **If you're in a hurry,** shopping at an outlet may be frustrating. Sizes and stock can be limited.

• **If you're short on cash,** an outlet store that doesn't take credit cards won't work. You may want to plan ahead for next season by putting aside an allotted amount of money each month.

• **Most outlets won't let you return goods**—a problem if you have a nasty habit of changing your mind frequently after you have purchased an item.

Factory Warehouse Outlets

Factory warehouse outlets are no longer the well-kept secret of informed bargain hunters. Today you can buy many source books telling you where to shop a factory outlet anywhere in the country (see page 154). Armed with the knowledge of where to shop, you can take advantage of the savings offered by factory outlet stores too.

The first time I went to a factory outlet store, I felt like

Tactics for Shopping Discount Outlet Stores

1. Know current retail prices before you shop an outlet and ask what the average discount is.

2. Find an outlet that sells designer and name-brand clothing. These outlets will offer you the best quality for your discounted dollar.

3. Combine your outlet shopping with other sources and you can save on all wardrobe fronts. It's difficult to fill all your shopping needs at one outlet.

4. Shop outlets frequently in the beginning of each buying season. This will help you find the best selection of merchandise and sizes. This is especially important when buying for children. Back-to-school fashions sell fast in August.

5. Check out the shopping tactics in the "Designer Discount Store" section (page 75). The same tactics will save you time, trouble and money when shopping at outlet stores.

Sherlock Holmes in pursuit of Professor Moriarty in the back streets of London. There I was, alone, taking a dingy freight elevator to an unknown territory that housed a coat manufacturing firm. When I reached my destination, an elderly woman asked what I wanted. I replied uncertainly, "I came to look for a coat." She led me to a back room where 20 coats were hanging under a dirty black window. I didn't find a coat that day, but it was such an adventure that I returned many times—only never alone!

As you can see, this is hit-or-miss shopping and requires energy and a desire to find a good deal. This section is designed to give you the factory outlet shopping tips you need to conserve your time and energy along with saving money.

Background

Manufacturers often sell merchandise directly to consumers through their own retail stores. These stores are called factory warehouse outlets, factory outlets or manufacturers' courtesy stores. A true factory outlet is one that's directly owned and operated by the manufacturer, near the manufacturer's factory. Some manufacturers are banding together and opening outlets in outlet shopping malls. Reading, Pennsylvania, is known as the "Factory Outlet Capital of the U.S.A."

Factory Warehouse Outlet Policies

Savings...........20–80% off list
Credit.............checks with ID
  (some); cash
Returns.......................none
Lay-bys........................none
Services.........minimal (wear form-fitting clothes for trying on things when there's no dressing room; bring bags for your purchases)
Displays........unglamorous— self-service shopping!
Stock..............often limited in sizes, styles

Factory outlets give the clothing manufacturers a place to sell their mistakes (irregulars or seconds), overruns, samples, discontinued styles and extra fabrics. The merchandise is sold at very low prices.

- **How to find one:** look in the source directory (see page 159), check the list of buying-guide books (see page 154) and skim the yellow pages (*Factory Outlets*).

Common clothing finds

- **Each outlet usually specializes in a particular clothing line:** men's suits, women's coats, girls' dresses, shoes and so on. You'll find name-brand manufacturers such as Florence Eiseman, Carter, Palm Beach, Levi, Evan Picone and Hush Puppies selling goods at their outlets across the country.

- **First quality items** include manufacturers' overruns or discontinued styles. Your current fashion knowledge will help you sort out the up-to-date merchandise.

- **Seconds and irregular merchandise** will be marked, but flaws may not be bad enough to affect the performance of the outfit. You'll have to determine this as you shop.

- **Bolts and pieces of material** left from the manufacturing process are often sold in factory outlets, making them great places for home seamstresses to buy fabric for less.

Tactics for Shopping Factory Outlet Stores

1. Do your homework and know current clothing prices before you shop. Most factory outlets won't give you the regular retail price on the merchandise tag. Your knowledge will help you determine your real saving percentage.

2. Phone a factory outlet before you shop. Ask questions about their store policies. Will they accept a check or credit card? Do they have your size? What hours are they open? Get directions to the outlet.

3. Put a limit on your budget before you get to the outlet and try hard to stick to it. This will help you from being overwhelmed if the store offers a lot of merchandise. However, if you find something you really need and want, don't pass it up. This is on-the-spot shopping—the item probably won't be available next time you visit.

4. Shop when you have lots of time. Keep yourself alert, flexible and curious. If you can, shop with a friend who shares the spirit of adventure. The two of you will have a ball!

5. Shop a large factory outlet as you would a supermarket. Systematically walk up and down each aisle. Pick up all the items that interest you. Then when you're finished, go to a corner and sort through your finds. Make a decision on what you do and don't want to purchase. Be sure to try on clothes for size, since there are no returns.

6. Make a thorough check of any garment before you buy. Turn clothes inside out and systematically inspect seams, try zippers and look over the fabric for any defects. If an item is marked *irregular, second,* or *as is,* make sure you know why. If you can't find the reason, ask a salesperson for help.

7. Don't shy away from a flawed item—just be sure the garment can still perform well with the flaw. Irregulars and seconds will be plentiful at factory outlets.

Advantages

• **If you get a feeling of adventure** when you're stalking an unknown bargain, factory warehouse shopping will be great fun for you.

• **If you are willing to spend more time than money** when shopping for clothes, you'll be more than satisfied with the money you save shopping at factory outlets.

• **If you sew,** you'll be delighted by the savings in fabric. Often this is material that's currently being shown in outfits at the better department stores.

Disadvantages

• **If you don't drive,** a factory outlet may be out of your reach. The majority of these outlets are located off the familiar retail path. And unless you travel all over, you're stuck with whatever garment industry is present locally.

Sample Shops

Twenty years ago many enterprising wives of clothing salesmen, and even the salesmen themselves, would sell garment samples out of their homes. News spread through neighborhoods about the good clothing buys at so-and-so's house. The demand was so great that many of these home ventures became another element in the retail clothing business.

Today's sample stores give you an immediate markdown on new clothes. You don't have to plan your shopping around seasonal sales. It's a great place for a busy buyer who wants to save a little money and lots of time. For the very determined bargain hunter, though, a sample shop may not reduce the retail price enough to give you that sense of saving (except during sale times). Read the following tips to see how you can use this clothing source to your shopping advantage.

Background

Sample shops are places where sales representatives' clothing is sold below the retail store price (goods are bought from many salespeople representing many manufacturers). These stores specialize in women's and children's clothing—men's sample stores are not that common. Most stores are located in neighborhoods away from the shopping malls and downtown areas. This is their concession to the retailer who may be selling the same goods for 30% more. If retail sources don't order a particular style, the sample becomes a one-of-a-kind outfit. Clothing is displayed neatly and attractively.

- **How to find one:** look in the yellow pages (*Women's Apparel* and *Children's and Infants' Wear*). The store will include "sample shop" in its name.

Sample Shop Policies

Savings..............30% off list; 30% more during sales
Credit..................bank credit cards, checks with ID, cash
Returns...........usually none; some exchange policies
Lay-bys....................usually
Pricing........tags should show retail and discount price—be sure the retail price isn't inflated
Announcements.........community newspapers, mailings (get on the list when you shop), word of mouth

Common clothing finds

- **Look for women's separates:** sportswear, suits, skirts, slacks, sweaters, evening clothes and accessories. Sizes are limited to 7,8,9,10 and 12. If you're a size 10, you are a perfect sample-shop size: you will find the best selection of clothes.

- **Look for children's better clothing:** girls' dresses, boys' suits and play clothes for both sexes. The most common sizes are for the age groups between two and eight.

Advantages

• **If you wear a small size,** you can save money on name-brand clothes in current styles.

• **If you need an outfit early in the season,** before the retail stores put their goods on sale, you can save money and have it to wear all season long. This applies to children's school clothes too.

• **If you prefer individuality in your clothes,** you can shop sample stores and find outfits that are not mass-manufactured. And you won't have to pay an arm and a leg for that exclusivity.

• **If you feel you have no fashion sense,** a sample shop offers color-coordinated separates to help make your selection simple.

Disadvantages

• **Unfortunately, if you're a man, or if you're a woman and you wear a size larger than 12,** you won't have much luck at most sample stores. But you should still scout your area for a sample shop that specializes in what you need. You may get lucky! Large-size sample shops are becoming more common; perhaps men's sample shops will too.

• **If you want to save a good amount of money on clothing,** you'll be disappointed by sample-shop prices. You'll be happier shopping retail sales, designer discount stores and second-hand sources.

Tactics for Shopping Sample Shops

1. If you find a store you like, ask to be put on the customer mailing list and you will be notified of upcoming sales.

2. Ask also to be put on a personal call list. Then if you prefer a certain manufacturer's clothes or are looking for a particular item, the store personnel will call you as soon as it comes in.

3. Bring along clothes you want to match when you go to a sample shop. Sales are final, so also be sure to try on clothes before you buy.

4. Ask if the store has a markdown area. Sometimes it's tucked away in the basement. Check this section first to save more money.

5. Pass by the accessories when you're shopping at a sample shop. You can get a better buy on these items elsewhere (discount chain stores or second-hand sources).

6. Merchandise is very current in styling at sample stores—it is the salesman's most current line of clothes. This means that some of the colors and styles will be trendy. If you're looking for clothes that will last, look through the racks carefully and choose the classic styles (see page 42).

7. There's no bargaining on prices. If you find a flaw you can certainly try to get the price down, but sample-shop people don't like to dicker.

Salesmen's Sample Garage Sales

The samples that clothing manufacturers' sales representatives show to the retail stores are often sold later in garage sales at the salesmen's homes. You can shop a salesman's sample garage sale and find clothes that have never been worn, at second-hand prices.

Background

This type of garage sale is full of new merchandise. It has sample clothing and accessories that the salesman has been showing to retail stores. There's no gimmick—you can buy new items without the retail mark-up and yet the seller still makes a profit.

• **How to find one:** watch your newspaper's classified ads (*Miscellaneous Sales*). The ads will read "salesman's sample sale" (and then list what's being sold).

Salesmen's Sample Garage Sale Policies

Savings............50–95% off list
Credit.......check with ID, cash
Returns..............usually none

Common clothing finds

• **Whatever the manufacturer's representative specializes in selling.** You could come across a sale of ski jackets, purses, children's clothing, men's suits or women's better sportswear.

Tactics for Shopping Salesmen's Sample Garage Sales

1. Buy out-of-season only when you know for sure you will make use of the garment or accessory in the proper season.

2. Check the clothing construction as a precaution before you buy. Remember the no return rule!

3. Bargaining is minimal, but you can try. After all, there's still a good profit margin for the seller. Ask how much the seller is willing to come down on the price.

Advantages

• **If you generally need what the salesman is selling,** go to the sale. If you find exactly what you need, you'll save money.

Disadvantages

• **If you are looking for a particular item,** you may not find a sale during the time of your wardrobe need.

Mail Order Shopping

Shopping by mail is fun and convenient . . . and sometimes the arrival of a long-awaited purchase is just what you need to brighten your day. You won't necessarily save a lot of money—although you can if you order through a wholesale catalog—but you *will* save time, gas and mileage.

Get in the mail order mood. Grab a cup of coffee, curl up in a favorite chair and read these mail order tips. You'll be in the perfect posture for shopping at home.

Background

Mail order companies issue catalogs describing their merchandise. You sit at home and decide what you want to buy. Almost anything can be ordered through the mail; sometimes it's the only way to find an unusual item.

The price of gasoline and the increasing number of people working full-time are two reasons we are seeing a mail order boom.

• **How to get catalogs:** look in the advertisement sections in the back of fashion magazines (see page 153). If friends get sent catalogs you like, jot down the firm's address and write for a copy. Once you're on their list, you'll probably never get off, and you'll most likely also begin receiving other companies' mailings as well. Also check the mail order sources list (see pages 155-158) for additional catalogs.

Common clothing finds

• **Some mail order firms specialize** and only offer men's clothes, for instance. Classic clothes, outdoor clothes and military surplus clothing are common mail order categories. Other firms sell clothing for everyone.

• **You can find listings of unique items,** from Western wear to hand-embroidered neckties.

• **Custom mail order firms** will manufacture clothing to your specification.

• **You may find wholesale prices** when ordering from some mail order firms, especially from foreign countries. For example, you can order Fair Isle sweaters from Scotland for $36.00 or cashmere sweaters from Hong Kong for $24.00.

Mail Order Catalog Policies

Savings ....30-70% off list from wholesale catalogs; up to list *plus* handling charges for some items—shop carefully!

Charges for catalogs ..rarely exceeds $5.00 (many are free); charge may be deducted from your first order

Credit ....bank credit cards; checks; money orders or cash not recommended because they can't be cancelled in case of problems and are stealable. Checks may be held for two weeks until they clear.

Foreign orders ....pay by International Money Order (get at a Post Office)

C.O.D. ....you may need to send a deposit; pay with cash or certified check when goods arrive

Special policies ......should be printed in the catalog near the ordering information

Insurance ....may be included in handling fees; add when optional if you prefer

Tactics for Shopping With Catalogs

1. Be familiar with your local retail prices. You can then determine whether you're really saving or paying the same amount as you would for retail. Weigh the time advantage against the cost, too. With unique items, you may not be able to compare costs. Maybe another mail order firm carries the item, though, even if no local stores stock it—so make your comparisons whenever you can.

2. Follow all ordering instructions in the catalog carefully.

3. Phone the mail order firm, if a WATS line is available, and let them answer your questions immediately. Any number with an 800-prefix instead of an area code is a toll-free number.

4. If you find a name-brand garment in a catalog, you may want to go to a local store first to try on that outfit. This will help you determine your correct size.

5. Update your catalogs. If yours is a year old, prices will probably have increased. Write the company and request a new one.

6. To order wholesale items by mail, refer to the source directory. Check out *The Wholesale by Mail Catalog* (see page 153).

7. Set aside a place at home for your mail order correspondence and receipts. Your proofs of payment, dates you ordered merchandise, and other data will be easier to locate if your order doesn't arrive. And if you're dissatisfied, your returns and refunds will go faster if your paperwork is centralized.

8. If nobody is home during the day to sign for UPS or other shipments, make arrangements *before* your items arrive. Call UPS and ask for a few receipts you can pre-sign (if your delivery man can leave the parcels someplace safe), or arrange for a neighbor to accept goods and sign for them. Another possibility is to have goods shipped to your place of work.

Advantages

• **If you are easy to fit** and wear an average size, you could easily order your whole wardrobe through the mail.

• **If you are short on time,** hate to go shopping and love getting items in the mail, you are a natural candidate for shopping at home. You will find the convenience a time and energy saver too. And if you're homebound, do not drive, or live in a location that is not near a major shopping area, home shopping is definitely the answer for you.

• **If you miss buying an outfit,** mail order shopping can help you out. Mail order firms keep items in stock longer than stores do.

Disadvantages

• **Mail order shopping may be too tame** for you if

you love to shop and ferret out bargains.

• **If patience is not your long suit,** mail order may be too much of a wait. Most deliveries do take a minimum of two weeks.

Retail Store Catalogs

If you haven't picked up a Sears', Penney's or Ward's catalog lately, you're going to be surprised. The photographic quality of the layouts is enticing and you can distinguish colors accurately. Fitting instructions are detailed in a way that makes it easier to get a correct fit. The styles are current, and there are many extra time-saving services.

This section will familiarize you with all the catalog shopping tips you'll need to make it simple to shop by phone.

Background

Sears, Penney's and Ward's have catalog services that offer all types of merchandise for every family member. All you have to do is sit back, study the catalog at your leisure and then pick up your phone and order.

You can shop by mail, phone or in person. Have your order mailed to you, delivered to your home or labeled for pickup at the store's catalog department.

If you are not a regular customer, you can walk into a store's catalog department and pay about $2.00 plus tax for a catalog. This amount can be

---

Retail Catalog Policies

Savings...............10–20% off catalog *store's* prices; more during sales
Credit.......store charge cards, bank credit cards, checks with ID, cash
Returns..........................yes
Rainchecks...................yes

---

deducted later from your first purchase.

• **At Ward's,** if you make three orders every six months, you're eligible for their Spring/Summer and Fall/Winter catalogs. You'll also receive the Christmas book and sale catalogs.

• **At Sears,** you must order about $25.00 every three months to receive the Spring/-Summer and Fall/Winter catalogs. You'll also receive the Christmas book and sale supplements.

• **At Penney's,** you must make two catalog orders, totaling $30.00, every six months. You'll then receive their Spring/Summer and Fall/Winter catalogs plus the Christmas and sale catalogs.

• **If you order a great deal of merchandise** from the catalog each season, chances are your catalog will be automatically mailed to you.

• **If you only meet the minimum ordering requirements** as stated above, you'll probably receive a postcard by mail to bring into your nearest store and pick up your catalog. You can send that postcard back and request that your catalog be mailed, if you prefer.

Common clothing finds

• **All types of clothing for every family member:** coats, suits, shoes, work boots, ski wear, juniors' sizes, children's clothes and infants' wear. The catalog service actually offers you more merchandise than you can find in the retail store.

• **Special catalogs:** Sears and Penney's offer special catalogs for uniforms, Western wear and clothes for big and tall men. Check on these. Each regular store catalog offers sizes in clothes and shoes for hard-to-fit people: husky boys; chubby girls; people who need half-sizes, extra-width shoes or special undergarment foundations.

Advantages

• **If you're short on time,** store catalog shopping makes it easy for you to order—by phone, by mail or in person. You can even have your orders delivered to your home.

Tactics for Shopping With Store Catalogs

1. Before placing your first order, read the yellow catalog information section thoroughly. This will familiarize you with all the store policies, services, ordering instructions and sizes. Don't overlook this section.

2. Use the fabric information chart in that section too. Then when you find a garment you like, read the fabric content and refer to the fabric chart. This will explain what you can expect from the fabric for durability and care.

3. Select the best quality for your money. Carefully read each garment description. Look for items that are made of wool blends, cotton blends or 100% natural fabrics (see pages 30–33).

4. Check out the regular store merchandise to help you order from the catalog. Many items in the store are in the catalog too. You can get an idea of sizes, colors, styles and the feel of fabric before you order.

5. Keep track of the brands and sizes that work well for you. Look for these the next time you order.

6. Save yourself interest charges by paying by check or money order when you're having items mailed or delivered. Otherwise you'll be paying interest on shipping costs and sales tax.

7. Gather all your needs before you order. Consolidated ordering will save you time and costs.

8. Buy back-to-school clothes in early August from the back-to-school sale supplement. You'll save money and avoid the pre-school rush in the stores.

9. If possible, pick up orders during dinner time. Stores are less crowded from 5:30 to 7:00 p.m.

- **If you're buying for many family members,** catalog shopping can offer a one-stop service.

Disadvantages

- **Store catalog shopping will not offer brand names or designer clothes.** However, you may still want to order minor items or children's clothes.

- **If you have bad luck getting your correct size** when ordering through catalogs, you'll probably shy away from this type of shopping. However, remember that you can always return the item.

Discount Shoe Stores

A really good deal on shoes is hard to come by. It requires searching for shoe discounters and patience while you wait for your favorites to go on sale. When you shop for shoes on discount, you must know good quality or you'll end up spending almost the full retail price of a pair of quality shoes for a lower-quality pair.

This spring, I did my closet appraisal and decided that I needed a pair of medium-heel pumps in beige or taupe.

My first stop was at a shoe discount store. I did a quick survey of the stock and noticed they carried many of last year's styles along with this year's shoes. But looking further, I found just what I wanted—a pair of taupe Joyce leather pumps, discount-priced at $20.00 and originally priced at $48.00. As a prepared shopper, I came away with a good discount on a pair of fashionable, quality shoes.

Remember that whenever you shop discount stores for clothes or shoes, you must be able to select this year's styles from last year's close-outs. These tips will help you shop discount shoe stores and get the most for your money.

Background

There are several types of discount shoe stores. Quality, prices and kinds of shoes in stock vary from store to store. A sample shoe store stocks small sizes for women or men. These high quality shoes are bought from salesmen's samples. Other shoe discounters are owned by large companies and have chain-store networks across the country. These discounters buy manufacturers' overruns, cancelled orders and store overstocks.

One large discounter, Payless Shoe Source, is affiliated with the May Company in California, a better department store. Payless puts its own name on shoes that are manufactured for them. Some of these shoes are made by better name-brand manufacturers. The shoes are identical in quality, but have the Payless label instead of their name-brand label. At Payless, a Nike tennis shoe is called a Pro Wings shoe; the savings is approximately 40%.

Some discount shoe stores are privately owned and buy overstocks, discontinued styles, seconds, cancelled orders—you name it. These stores stock a variety of brand names and designer shoes at different times.

• **How to find one:** look in the yellow pages (*Shoes*), check the source directory in this book (see page 159), and watch for newspaper ads.

Common shoe finds

• **You'll find men's, women's and children's footwear**—casual shoes, cowboy boots, athletic shoes, and dressy shoes. You will see well-known brand names as well as discount store brand names.

• **Some shoes will look dated** (be sure you know current styles and can pick out the classic look) and many shoes will be in man-made materials rather than leather. Go for the leather. Read the writing inside the shoe to be sure of what you're getting.

Discount Shoe Store Policies

Savings...........20–40% off list in season; up to 65% at sales; up to 75% on seconds and out-of-season shoes
Credit.........bank credit cards (at some), check with ID, cash
Returns..........within 14 days
Lay-bys.......................none
Services.......varies (most are self-serve; some have clerks)
Rainchecks.....yes, on store's own brands
Stock..........arrives weekly at some stores (ask when and shop when new things arrive)

Tactics for Shopping Discount Shoe Stores

1. Know what's currently in style so you can spot an expensive pair of shoes.

2. Do your homework on quality by exploring expensive shoe stores first. Read the writing inside the shoes and on the soles. Learn the feel of leather. When you see "all parts are man-made," that means none of it is leather. If it reads "leather uppers," then just the outside of the shoe is leather, while the sole and inside are man-made. A very expensive shoe has even the bottom sole made of leather.

3. Examine expensive, well-made athletic shoes to familiarize yourself with quality too. This will also help you recognize a shoe that is made by a better manufacturer but that carries a discount store label. Ask clerks if you are not sure about it. They will freely tell you who makes what. If you're after good footwear investments, choose classic styles (see page 45) and neutral colors that will work for at least three seasons. This will give you more performance for your money.

Advantages

• **If you're looking for a trendy shoe** that you won't wear often—where durability doesn't count—a discount shoe store can be a sensible shopping source.

• **If you have the time to ferret out a quality shoe,** go to a discount shoe store. You can find footwear in season at reduced prices, so you won't have to wait for store clearance sales.

• **If you're buying shoes for a fast-growing family,** be sure to check a discount shoe store first.

Disadvantages

• **If you're looking for a specific style, have a hard-to-fit size, or have special foot problems,** discount shoe stores will not be easy shopping sources for you. It will probably be worth it to you to pay more for your shoes elsewhere.

Close-Out Stores

Just to put you in the mood for this type of shopping, let me tell you about one of my visits to a close-out store. It was at one of the Pic'n'Save stores in California. There were several racks of Danskin leotards that day, selling for $4.99—a 66% discount. When I started out shopping, I had no thought of buying a leotard, but I needed one. At that price I figured I might as well get one, so I did!

Close-out stores can be a delight to the novice and veteran bargain hunter alike. They offer large lots of one-time-only merchandise. The shopping is completely unpredictable, so you never know what great things you'll find, but chances are you'll find that whatever's there is very cheap. Here are some tips to arouse your curiosity and put you on the close-out bargain trail.

Background

Close-out stores buy at rock-bottom prices from manufacturers who, for a variety of reasons, are anxious to unload their merchandise. The items may be discontinued merchandise; they may have bombed in the retail stores; or they may be manufacturers' overstock. Items may also come from retail stores that are in a hurry to liquidate leftover merchandise or are going bankrupt. All the merchandise is sold reasonably to the consumer. Merchandise can change daily, weekly or monthly, never to be back in the store again.

• **How to find one:** look in the yellow pages (*Department Stores*). Check newspaper ads and ask friends and neighbors if they have ever shopped a close-out store.

Close-Out Store Policies

Savings..........40–80% off list
Credit........most are cash only
Returns.....................varies
Services..................minimal

Common clothing finds

• **You'll find all types of clothing** (as well as other merchandise at one time or another), but you'll never know what to expect. On a good day, you could see name-brand and designer clothing, though sizes, colors and stock may be limited. Look for accessories and brand-name children's clothing for real savings.

Advantages

• **If you have time and energy,** it's fund to browse through a close-out store. If you do this a couple of times a month, you're bound to happen on items you need, at very reasonable prices.

• **If you're shopping for everyday clothing items,** a close-out store is a good first place to check. Very often they stock underwear, sports gear, eye make-up, shaving cream—basic items. You can't be specific about brands you're after or you'll be disappointed.

Disadvantages

• **If you're short on time,** you'll just be frustrated shopping at a close-out store. The selection is too unpredictable and limited to pay off.

Tactics for Shopping Close-Out Stores

1. Shop frequently if you're really going to capitalize on the savings at this type of store. Before you buy, ask yourself if you really need the item. Don't feel that you must buy something every time you go.

2. Beware of faddish items that are already out-of-date even at reduced prices.

3. Inspect the racks with the brand-name and designer merchandise first. Read labels and fabric content carefully.

Damaged Goods Stores

A damaged goods store offers soup-to-nuts shopping—but never the whole meal at once! You'll find the most unusual merchandise thrown together. At Bank's, a store in Minneapolis, Minnesota, that sells damaged goods for insurance companies, I once found frozen fish—along with an Anne Klein blazer. It's illogical and irreverent, yes, but definitely interesting. Crazy combinations occur frequently in such places.

You must be a careful, energetic shopper when you visit a damaged goods store. The bargains abound for those with keen eyes. (By the way, that Anne Klein blazer cost me $20.00, though the original price was $180.00.) Come with a curious eye, a good sense of humor and lots of patience, and you'll have a great time.

Background

Damaged goods stores buy merchandise from anxious manufacturers and stores when their stock has been damaged in shipping or by fires, floods and other acts of God and man. A few damaged goods companies sell only for insurance firms. They have buyers out in the field that almost literally follow fire trucks, and then go in and help the insurance company unload the losses. These companies may sell the merchandise right on the spot or may transfer it to their stores.

These stores can also be called salvage stores, surplus stores or unclaimed freight stores.

You can expect them to be short on atmosphere and long on variety.

• **How to find one:** most damaged goods stores advertise their merchandise under *Miscellaneous Sales* in the classified ads section of the newspaper and don't advertise in the phone book's yellow pages, since they try to keep their overhead low.

Damaged Goods Store Policies

Savings...........40–80% off list (though some of the goods are damaged and thus not worth full list price)

Credit.........bank credit cards (at some), checks with ID, cash

Returns......................none

Lay-bys......................none

Services..................minimal

Damage....goods meet federal standards and are cleaned and disinfected before being stocked—if you still smell smoke, don't buy

---

Common clothing finds

• **Not all damaged goods stores sell clothes.** Their ads in the newspaper classified section will tell you the type of merchandise currently available.

• **Stock varies enormously.** Depending on quirks of fate, you can expect to occasionally find name-brand and designer clothes at damaged goods stores. Look for men's sport-coats, women's blazers, children's play clothes, ski wear, wedding gowns, underwear, shoes and jewelry. You name it: eventually they'll have it. The merchandise is often current in style and sold in the proper season.

• **Damage.** You'll find that some of the clothes are smoke-damaged, water-damaged, spotted or torn. But not all of the merchandise will have been affected by the catastrophe. The undamaged goods will be sold along with the damaged stock, but you'll pay more for them if they are in perfect condition.

Advantages

• **If you're a veteran bargain hunter,** you'll love this type of shopping atmosphere. It's a real thrill to locate and sort out the winning merchandise.

• **If you regularly read the store's classified ads,** you'll have a chance to buy at a real saving when the store offers items you need. This is great when you have the extra shopping time it takes.

Disadvantages

• **If you're short on time,** don't even consider shopping at damaged goods stores. The returns on your time aren't going to pay off.

• **If you're planning to build a wardrobe or make major purchases,** don't rely on damaged goods stores. Combine this source with many others.

Tactics for Shopping Damaged Goods Stores

1. Check the classified ads daily to keep up on the store's changing stock and special sales.

2. When a sale begins, go the night before and take a sneak preview as the merchandise is being put out. You probably won't be able to buy, but you'll get a good look at the goods and know where they will be located the next day.

3. Plan to wait in line before the door opens on the days of special sales. This is a very hectic time to shop. I usually go later that day, around the dinner hour. By then the stock has been regrouped on the shelves, the salespeople have recovered and I can take time to carefully inspect the merchandise. Many times during the first rush of a sale, good merchandise gets overlooked.

4. Know current retail prices. Then weigh the percentage you save against the chance you take when you buy damaged goods. You should be saving at least 50% if the item is wearable "as is," but you should be saving 75% if you need to repair the garment.

5. Take your time when shopping. You'll need to inspect everything very carefully. Smell the clothes to be sure there's no leftover smoke odor. Check hemlines and fabric for any water damage. Turn the garment inside out and look for color runs from humidity damage. When there's a large shipment of goods, ask a salesperson what the damaging circumstances were. If you can find out, it will help in your inspection.

6. Keep a sharp eye for minor repairs and slight spotting. Sometimes the markdown on these items is so great that you can take a chance on getting them fixed.

7. Shop at times when shoes or jewelry or any items that aren't easily damaged are offered. These will be your best bets.

Finding Second-Hand Clothes For Less

Some people don't feel comfortable about wearing previously owned garments. When I was managing a thrift store, new customers would come in to buy furniture or glassware, never intending to look at the clothes. I would size them up and pick out an outfit I thought they might like or which might fit them. They were always amazed that something so good-looking was available at such a low price.

One day a woman bought a pair of Florsheim pumps in near-new condition. The fit was perfect; the cost, $3.00. She kept remarking to her friend, "I've never bought second-hand clothes before and can't believe I'm buying a pair of second-hand shoes." Her companion finally said, "You would be a fool not to buy them."

You'll find bargains at second-hand clothes sources that are virtually there for the grabbing. This chapter will transform you into a well-educated second-hand shopper before you even leave the house. You will know where to buy, how much money you can save, the policies at all the various sources, the pros and cons of each source and inside buying tips for whatever type of shopping arena you choose.

The key to dressing better for less is to choose the best quality at every shopping source. When you're buying second-hand, this is especially important, whether the item costs 50¢ or $15.00. *Always* select the "good stuff."

Before you shop any second-hand source, be sure to read Chapter Three, so you'll know a real bargain when you see one. Also read Chapter Six, so you can determine which second-hand items can be easily updated or altered.

My Second-Hand Story

Two years ago I conducted a personal clothes-buying experiment. My goal was to see if I could dress fashionably, spend very little money and buy only second-hand clothes. I did this for one year. At that time I was working as a television producer. My job required that I dress professionally and with style. Being a producer demanded a great deal of my time, so I was limited to shopping right after work or on Saturdays.

Criteria

Here are the criteria I set for myself. One hard-set rule was that I would *not* allow myself to buy any clothes from a new source for one year (this included clothes on sale or at discount prices). Instead, I shopped a variety of second-hand sources—rummage sales, garage sales, thrift stores and resale shops.

My second rule was that the clothes had to be in current style. I wanted to look like I had stepped out of a fashion magazine.

For my third rule, I vowed I would not spend more than $20.00 for one item, no matter how good a bargain it was or how much I wanted the outfit.

Questions

When I finished the year's experiment, I wanted to be able to answer these questions: Is it possible to dress fashionably just using second-hand clothing sources? Could I feel confident in my wardrobe image? How much time and energy would I need to spend searching out the bargains? How much could I really save?

Here are my answers to those questions. I received more compliments on my clothes than I ever had in the past. People were constantly asking me where I bought my outfits. I delighted in watching their expressions when I told them I bought a complete outfit at a garage sale for $1.50.

My job gave me a lot of visibility in the community. Only once did I feel unsure of an outfit I was wearing. I attended a play and wore a black crepe 1940's dress with all the proper accessories, including a veiled hat and gloves. The complete outfit cost me less than $8.00. I felt excited about the buys, but couldn't personally pull off the look. After that experience, I stuck with the classics.

Time savings

When I first started shopping exclusively for second-hand clothes, it required more of my time than I could afford to spend. So I took on the added challenge of shopping in the shortest time possible. I persevered and as my shopping skills increased, I found I was spending less time than I ever had when I was shopping for new clothes. I was able to judge just by the newspaper ads what garage sales not to attend. I could shop an entire rummage sale in 35 minutes or survey a resale shop in 15 minutes. And I discovered what thrift stores in town were worth shopping and when the best time to shop was. Even when I was shopping for a specific item, I was able to find it quickly.

Money savings

I saved a *lot* of money. My credit cards sat idle for a year. I owed nothing! Here's a description and the cost of the basic second-hand work wardrobe I purchased during that year.

- **Two coats.** One three-season white wool coat bought at a thrift store. Cost: $10.00. One winter mouton fur coat bought at a garage sale. Cost: $1.75.

- **Two 1940's tailored women's suits,** bought at a garage sale. Cost: $1.50 apiece.

- **Two blouses.** One silk Charlotte Ford blouse bought at

a resale store. Cost: $12.00. The other, a rayon 1950's round-collared blouse bought at a rummage sale. Cost: 50¢.

• **One pair of gabardine slacks** bought at a thrift store. Cost: $4.00. I had the slacks altered at a cost of $8.00, making the total investment $12.00.

• **One Shetland wool cardigan sweater** bought at a garage sale. Cost: $1.00.

• **One wool tweed College Town blazer** bought at a garage sale. Cost: $3.50.

• **Two pairs of shoes.** One pair of Charles Jourdan black ballet pumps bought at a resale store. Cost: $5.00. One pair of perfect condition, T-strap Capezio flat shoes bought at a Salvation Army store. Cost: 50¢.

TOTAL COST: $49.25

This wardrobe took me to meetings, through work on-camera, and out to evenings on the town after work. My satisfaction with the experiment was double, because I knew I looked better dressed than I ever had before—and I had paid virtually nothing for my improved wardrobe.

So even if you've never shopped for second-hand clothes, you owe it to yourself to try the thrill of finding your own bargains. (Not to mention the thrill you'll have at saving money, besides.) Give it a try!

Second-Hand Shopping Tools

Bring along the following tools when you shop at the second-hand sources.

☐ **Want-ad clippings.** Clip the newspaper want ads for garage sale and rummage sale locations. Bring these with you to help you find the sales.

☐ **Area map.** Some second-hand sources may be located in out-of-the-way places. A map can save you time in unknown territory.

☐ **Magnet.** A great help in determining whether an item is brass, gold or copper. If the magnet does *not* adhere to the item, it's not made of a cheap metal. It's probably what it looks like—either brass, gold or copper.

☐ **Magnifying glass.** Useful when you are examining jewelry. You will be able to read the gold or silver content.

☐ **Measuring tape.** Great for quickly determining size. Many second-hand clothes have lost their size tags.

☐ **Large hand-mirror.** Not all second-hand sources provide mirrors (and many that do don't have the winged kind that lets you see your back.)

☐ **Small flashlight.** This helps you to examine the condition of clothing when you are in badly lit areas: a garage, a thrift store or a basement rummage sale.

☐ **Notebook and pen.** Absolutely necessary when you attend an auction. At the merchandise preview beforehand you will want to make notes about the items you will bid for.

Quality Shopping Plan

To help you select the "good stuff" and ferret out the quality items, follow this shopping plan at any second-hand clothing source.

1. Before you go shopping, flip through fashion magazines (see page 153) and see what stores are showing in colors, patterns and style design. Take a look at current retail prices too. Apply this knowledge to your second-hand finds. You'll be more aware of the alteration possibilities and better able to spot a fashion repeat—a garment whose time has come again—when you find it.

2. If you are at a rummage sale or garage sale and are competing with many other shoppers, just grab items—don't stop to inspect them. Wait until you have scoured the whole sale. Then go through your finds and discard what you don't want.

3. Inspect items carefully. Look for quality in construction (see pages 27–30) and good fabric. Check all the stress points for good condition (see pages 98–99).

4. Read all clothing labels to help determine quality. To identify designer labels, use the classic manufacturers' chart as a guide (see page 47). In men's suits, you'll sometimes find the date the suit was bought on one of the inside pockets of the jacket. This will give you an idea of how old the suit is.

5. Read the fiber content labels. Go for the 100% silks, wools and cottons, or a good blend of natural fabrics and synthetic fiber. Sometimes fiber labels are missing. Train your hands to recognize the feel of good fabric by touch. Polyesters are shiny and slippery to the touch.

6. Try on everything you like. Sizes are often misleading or altogether missing on second-hand clothes. If the garment is too large, you may want to have it altered. Do this only when the fabric is excellent and the altering job is not major. You can make things smaller, but *not* larger (see page 130).

7. Go for the classic designs (see pages 42–47). In previously owned classic clothes, you'll find good performance the second time around. For example: Harris Tweed sportcoats, London Fog raincoats, cardigan sweaters and khaki trousers.

8. Shop second-hand sources first when a fad has returned (see pages 48–51). When it's a season of fashion repeaters (chemises, suspenders, Bermuda shorts), you'll find them in all sorts of second-hand sources.

9. Shop for all jewelry and accessories at second-hand sources first. You'll find better-quality items for less than you would pay for cheaply made items at discount chain stores.

Common Stress Points
in Second-Hand Garments

Inspect for the following stress areas before you buy second-hand clothes. If you find a flaw that can easily be fixed, use it as a bargaining tool and buy the item for even less.

Stress Areas	Fixable?
• Missing buttons.	Yes.
• Broken zippers.	Yes.
• Moth holes in sweaters.	Don't bother.
• Pilling on sweaters and wool fabric.	You may be able to remove it with a razor.
• Pilling on the inside collar of a man's shirt.	Don't bother if the abrasion is extensive.
• Frayed cuffs on shirt sleeves.	Yes, if you are going to make it into a short-sleeved shirt.
• Worn crotch and seat area on slacks and trousers.	Don't bother.
• Frayed area on front zipper flap of men's trousers.	Don't bother.
• Any seam area that's slightly ripped. Check all seams, especially under arms, suit vents, pockets and crotch.	Yes.
• Actual rip, hole or cigarette burn in the fabric.	Only if it's an area you want to patch.
• Fabric ripples in blazers or suitcoats around the collar and front area of the coat. Caused by improperly glued interfacing material.	No. Avoid this garment. The ripples do not press out, even professionally.
• Worn knees in jeans.	Yes, if you can add a patch or make cut-off shorts.
• Frayed material on the cuffs of pants. (You'll see this most often in children's slacks.)	Yes, if you're going to hem the slacks shorter or add trim.
• Worn elbows on sportcoats.	Yes, if they would look good with suede patches.

(continued)

Common Stress Points
in Second-Hand Garments *(continued)*

Stress Areas	Fixable?
• Worn lining and ripped lining in jackets, blazers or coats.	Yes, if the lining is wearable for one more season and the rips are in the seam. No, if you have to replace the whole lining.
• Ripped or worn pockets.	Yes.
• Old hemline marks on velvet or knit fabrics.	No, very few marks are easily removed from a previous hemline. Only buy when the price is cheap, and you're willing to take a chance. Refer to the stain chart (see pages 58–59).
• Down-filled jackets, when you can feel that the down has shifted considerably.	No.
• Wear on furs around the sleeve cuffs, pockets and front closure.	Yes, if you want to add a trim. Extensive wear in other areas can't be fixed.
• Stained or worn suede garments.	No.
• Rips in leather that are not extensive and are placed in a hidden area.	Yes, these can often be glued.
• Stains in the obvious spilling areas: on the fronts of shirts and dresses, the lap in slacks, the seat area and the cuffs of pants.	Sometimes, but first refer to the stain chart (see pages 58–59).
• Spots on men's ties.	Don't bother.
• Black ball-point pen stains.	No.
• Broken straps on shoes.	Yes, but only fix if the shoe is made of good leather and is reasonably priced.
• Salt stains on shoes and boots.	Yes. If the salt stain isn't too bad, you can remove it with a 50/50 solution of white vinegar and water.
• Perspiration stains on underarms.	No, especially in silk fabric.

Resale Stores

If you are a bit squeamish about wearing previously owned clothes, a good resale (consignment) shop will eliminate those fears. When I visited Michael's resale shop in Manhattan, I found designer day and evening clothes (with original price tags of thousands of dollars), worn once by their wealthy owners, being resold for $100.00 and $200.00.

Resale stores offer second-hand clothes shopping at its finest. They resemble small specialty stores. The clothes are clean and neatly displayed, and the selection is good. You'll get the impression that you're looking into a well-dressed friend's closet, for there will be very little wear showing on the garments. Many men buy their complete office wardrobes—suits, shirts and ties—at resale stores. I shop at resale stores when I am in a hurry and looking for a more expensive item (blazer, suit and so on), and pick up other items from other sources as I can.

Resale stores can combine men's, women's and children's clothes, or they may be specialized. This section will give you tips on shopping for men and women (see pages 102–103 for children's resale tips).

Background

Resale (consignment) stores are shops that sell second-hand clothing. People bring in their used clothing. The resaler examines the garments and judges whether they are good enough to resell, then prices the outfit and displays it just as a new retail clothing store does. The owner of the clothes gets 50% of the price when a garment sells; the store owner gets the other 50%. A successful resale store owner establishes fashion guidelines that all stock must meet and cultivates relationships with the wealthier men and women in a locale. These people discard their clothes after one wearing or one season, and thus they have great resale value. You'll be surprised at how many well-to-do men and women sell—and buy—at resale stores (and never tell!).

• **How to find one:** look in the yellow pages (*Clothing Bought and Sold, Second-Hand Stores, Thrift Stores* and *Women's* or *Men's Apparel.*)

Resale Store Policies

Savings...........65–85% off list
Credit..............check with ID, cash
Returns.......................none
Lay-bys................ask—some have them
Pricing................determined by the shop owner (clothes owner gets 50%); usually further discounts after 30 or 60 days
Cleaning.................items are supposed to be clean—let shop owner determine whether to adjust your price to include cleaning
Style.............items should be in style and in season

Tactics for Shopping Resale Stores

1. Remember: the stores only take in seasonal clothing. The best shopping times: September and October for fall and winter clothes; November for holidays; and April, May and June for spring and summer clothes.

2. Shop the resale stores frequently during the best times. You'll be at the store when incoming merchandise is put on the racks.

3. Get personally acquainted with the store personnel. Tell them the items you are looking for and ask to be put on a special customer list. Some stores will contact you when an appropriate outfit comes in.

4. Ask the salespeople about designer clothing, more expensive items and new arrivals. Sometimes stores keep these items behind the counter (or maybe an outfit is still sitting unmarked in a back room).

5. If a garment you find at a resale store has a manufacturer's label cut out, it's a good possibility that the item was originally bought at a designer discount or outlet store. So the markdown should be better than you could get at one of these other sources. You may want to ask the store personnel to lower the price to reflect the correct percentage discount from the original, discounted price. You'll be best able to do this if you have an up-to-date knowledge of current prices at all of these sources.

6. No matter what size you wear, don't just look in your size range. Second-hand clothes are not always true to their marked sizes.

7. Keep in mind alteration possibilities when you're looking at an outfit. If you don't sew yourself, ask the store personnel to recommend a seamstress or tailor.

8. Don't buy late in the season at a resale store. You can do better buying new clothes then at retail seasonal sales or at discount sale prices. The exceptions to this are the very expensive items, such as furs, and the year-round clothing, such as gabardine suits.

9. Inspect the clothing carefully before you buy. If you do find a flaw or feel the garment needs cleaning, use this to your bargaining advantage. But if the tag states that a garment is being sold "as is" or "needs cleaning," you will get nowhere trying to bargain. This means the price was adjusted to fit the problem. In general, bargaining is at a minimum at resale stores.

10. Ask the store personnel whether an item is ready to be marked down. Stores don't always stay on top of their 30- to 60-day markdowns. You may get the item for less than the tag price, or risk coming back to get it later when it's further discounted.

11. If you find an outfit or shoes that you really like and the fit is great, ask the salesperson questions about the person who brought the items in. Maybe he or she will be bringing in more items! If so, have the store call you.

Common clothing finds

• **Look for designer clothing for men and women:** men's and women's suits and better-quality clothing of all types, including shoes and accessories. Some resale stores may also have a small assortment of new clothing or samples.

Advantages

• **If you can find a resale store in your area with fast turnovers** in clothes of your size, you are in luck. You can dress in the best of fashion for less! I have found a resale store where I buy all my boots and shoes. Some wonderful woman wears my shoe size and only puts on her very expensive purchases three or four times before she tires of them and brings them to the resale shop. My last purchase there was a pair of Margaret Jerrold soft leather boots (in brand-new condition) for $35.00. At a retail store they would have cost $150.00.

Disadvantages

• **You may have to drive to an out-of-the-way place** to arrive at a resale shop. And if you like to dig for your bargains and save even more money, don't start your shopping at a resale store. The savings are less here than buying at a garage or rummage sale.

• **Some resale stores have relatively slow turnovers** of merchandise; they are worth only occasional visits.

Children's Resale Stores

The growing success of resale stores across the country coupled with the demand for good recycled kids' clothes has led to the opening of many children's resale stores. These stores are selective about the condition of the clothes they take in, and they offer growing families an easy shopping alternative to beat the high cost of children's clothes.

Background

Children's resale stores are very similar to other resale (consignment) shops except that they sell only children's merchandise. This merchandise is brought in by a previous owner, who pockets 50% of the marked price. In addition to clothing, these stores take and sell on consignment children's furniture, toys and accessories.

• **How to find one:** look in the yellow pages (*Clothing Bought and Sold* and *Second-Hand Stores.*) Ask friends with children.

Children's Resale Store Policies

Savings..........65–85% off list on the used and 30–60% off list on the sample clothes
Credit.............check with ID, cash
Returns ....usually none
Lay-bys.........ask about them
Pricing...............see page 100
Announcements ..ask about the mailing list for sales ads

Common clothing finds

- **New children's sample clothes along with second-hand stock.** You will find infant sleepers, blankets, pre-schoolers' play clothes and dress clothes. Boy scout and girl scout uniforms and sports equipment are also good buys. The sizes range from newborn to size 14. The selection diminishes past size 8, especially for boys' wear.

Advantages

- **If you are looking for better quality** or designer children's clothing for ages 1 through 8, you will save money buying second-hand at these stores. The shopping environment is pleasant and it's a place that can really save you time in picking up an outfit. It's also a great place to resell your own children's clothing. This is a real advantage when you consider how quickly children outgrow their clothes!

Disadvantages

- **If you are looking for a large selection,** sometimes the resale stores are limited. You may not be able to find the exact item of clothing that you need.

- **If your children are over 8 years,** the supply can be very limited. You may need to go to several stores to find clothing in larger sizes. Unfortunately, most children's resale stores are not located near each other, so you may have to use a little gas to get to the bargains.

Tactics for Shopping Children's Resale Stores

1. Phone the store ahead and ask if the items you want are in stock.

2. Familiarize yourself with prices. It isn't worth it to buy a Sears toddler outfit second-hand for $2.50 if it sells new in the Sears catalogue for $3.95.

3. Look for designer and better children's clothing labels such as Polly Flinders, Florence Eiseman, Ann Klein, Carter and Health-Tex.

4. Bring your finds to the salesperson and ask when they will be marked down. The 30- to 60-day markdown policy also applies here (see page 100).

5. Bargaining is marginal, but it never hurts to try, especially when clothes are stained or torn.

Goodwill/ Salvation Army Stores

If you assume that only people on extremely tight budgets shop at Goodwill/Salvation Army stores, you are in for a big surprise. If you consider yourself as part of the middle class, then you are part of the group that's a major source of customers for Goodwill/Salvation Army stores. These stores are flourishing during our inflationary times. They offer *real* bargains to determined money-conscious shoppers, especially the shoppers who know quality and brand-name labels. Speaking of labels, the Boston-area Goodwill stores have started sewing their own labels on jeans as a take-off on designer jeans. They label theirs "Morgies." The cost: $3.25.

Here's a story about someone who found a terrific bargain at a Salvation Army store. A friend of my father's who was visiting from out of town forgot to bring along his golf shoes. Dad took Jack to shop for a pair. When they pulled up in front of a Salvation Army store, Jack looked surprised and said, "What are we doing here?" My dad loved it and replied, "This is our first shopping stop for your golf shoes."

Jack found a pair of Foot Joys that had originally cost $85.00. They were in perfect condition, with all the cleats intact. Because Jack knew the value of good golf shoes, he was able to select the best at a very reasonable price: $8.00. You can learn how to do this too!

Background

These stores are run by charitable service organizations. All the merchandise is donated. Located in almost all cities in the United States and Canada, the stores vary in neatness and layout from location to location.

• **How to find one:** look in the yellow pages (*Clothing, Second-Hand Stores, Thrift Shops* and *Women's Apparel*). Look also in the white pages under Goodwill or Salvation Ar-

my (see page 159 for a list of cities with these sources).

Goodwill/Salvation Army Store Policies

Savings...........75–95% off list
Credit............checks with ID, cash
Returns.......sometimes—ask
Lay-bys........................none
Pricing..............usually done by the rack or table rather than by the item
Tax angles.............be sure to get a receipt for your donated clothes

---

Common clothing finds

• **Look for clothing for men, women and children.** You will find coats, suits, skirts, slacks, jeans, t-shirts and military garments. Most Goodwill stores have a "Treasure Room" with better jewelry, clothing and collectible glassware. Some Salvation Army stores have a specialty also.

• **Expect unique items at these stores.** My favorites include a pair of 1940's gold-washed sterling earrings that cost me $3.11. A pair of black silk slacks, originally from a Beverly Hills store, cost me $1.50. A silk 1930's Japanese jacket, in perfect condition, cost $5.00.

Advantages

• **If you know quality and are a real bargain trooper,** you can find many great outfits at a considerable savings in these stores.

Disadvantages

- **If you have little time or patience** for shopping, you will not enjoy digging and sorting through racks of marginal clothes to find that great outfit.

Tactics for Shopping Goodwill/Salvation Army Stores

1. Look for the best quality and the best condition items on a rack. You can pay $2.49 for junk or $2.49 for a jewel. You must know quality and current prices. Read labels every time you pick up a garment.

2. Pick up all the items you think you want until you're done shopping. Then ask yourself these questions: do I really need this item? Do I love it? Does it fit? Is it in good condition? If the answer is yes to all these questions, then buy. You probably won't find it in the store again if you put it back to think it over further.

3. Think in terms of how an outfit can be altered. If you find a pair of quality-fabric slacks that are out of style but fit, maybe you can update them.

4. Consider Goodwill/Salvation Army stores as sources for costumes at Halloween or for school plays. If you have a good imagination, you'll find a wealth of items to get those creative juices flowing.

5. If you sew, these stores can be a great clothes source. You can buy outfits cheaply just for their notions: fringe material, belts, fur collars. Or look for a box of odd buttons. You may find items you can cut other garments from as well.

Thrift Stores

I managed the Steeple People Thrift Store in Minneapolis, Minnesota, last year. Each Monday I would meet volunteers at the church basement and we would sort through the new donations. We never knew what surprises were waiting in the bags and boxes. But I was always amazed at the quality items people donated: silver jewelry, furs, Harris Tweed sportcoats, 100% silk blouses, London Fog raincoats. You have to see it to believe it!

Thrift stores are often packed with unique items, but the good merchandise goes immediately. The secret to making them work for you is to find a thrift store you like and shop the first few hours they are open every week.

Some people may be concerned that the volunteers or manager of a thrift store get the first grab at the best things. While this happens to a certain extent, the volume of donations is so overwhelming that the staff can't use or afford everything they see. And the people in charge are not always wise to the value of an item. Your real competition comes from dealers who know how to spot a good deal.

Background

Thrift stores are operated by service or church organizations. All of the merchandise is donated; the profits go for a charitable purpose. The Junior League of Women, for example, operates a "chain" of thrift stores across the country (see page 159).

• **How to find one:** look in the yellow pages (*Clothing, Second-Hand Stores, Thrift Shops* and *Women's Apparel*).

Thrift Store Policies

Savings...........75–95% off list
Credit......check with ID, cash
Returns.............usually none
Lay-bys..............usually none
Pricing.....................varies in fairness—know your values and compare shops

---

Common clothing finds

• **Look for a good cross-section of clothing for everyone:** men's suits, women's dresses, slacks, skirts and children's play clothes. Some stores even have what they call a "Designer Section" with better women's clothing, especially evening gowns. I love to pick through all the jewelry, scarves and accessories.

Advantages

• **If you love to rummage,** you will do plenty of it at a thrift store. If you like the excitement of never knowing what you may find, you will get that too at a thrift store. Whatever you buy, you can be sure the savings will be great!

Disadvantages

• **If you prefer orderly merchandise** when you shop, stay away from thrift stores. You will probably spend lots of time combing through racks of clothes, and you may not find a thing you want to buy.

Tactics for Shopping Thrift Stores

1. Get acquainted with the women's organizations in your city that may have thrift stores (see page 105). Some of the best designer clothes and expensive evening wear come out of thrift stores run by wealthier women's organizations.

2. Ask when the store gets restocked with new donations. Shop early on that day. If you can't find what you're looking for, ask the manager if it could be in the back room or stored elsewhere.

3. Check the clothes carefully for rips, stains or signs of wear. Donated clothing is not always clean.

4. Ask to be put on a list if you're looking for something special or if, for instance, you wear a special-size shoe. Some managers will call you when the item comes in.

5. Before you buy, check to see whether the item you want is going on sale soon (except when it's a hot-demand item—then grab it). Don't assume that a sale is going to include all merchandise. Sometimes the better items are removed to the back during a sale. Question the salesperson about what exactly will be on sale.

6. Bargain whenever you want. Most thrift store personnel expect it.

Estate Sales

Buying clothes at estate sales is hit-or-miss shopping that can take up a whole Saturday morning. But it's an exciting way to buy expensive outfits for less, especially if you like seeing other people's homes.

Background

Estate sales are run by professionals hired to appraise and sell the contents of a household. Quality merchandise is sold at higher prices than at garage sales, but goods are competitive with antique stores. Since clothes are of secondary interest (compared to furniture) for the dealers and buyers at estate sales, there are good deals to be found.

- **How to find one:** check classified newspaper ads (*Estate Sales* or *Household Goods*). Also look in neighborhood and community newspapers. Most ads will be in a bold, large print and will give the name of the dealer.

Estate Sale Policies

Savings...................65–90%, depending on quality and condition of clothes

Credit.....checks with ID, cash

Returns........................none

Lay-bys........................none

Pricing..............prices are set but bids are acceptable. Leave a bid and phone number behind for items you want.

Children..............don't bring them—not enough to hold their interest

Tactics for Shopping Estate Sales

1. If the ad reads that numbers will be given before the sale starts (bakery fashion), go early to get a low number or place in line.

2. Be patient. Sometimes only 15 people at a time are let into a sale. Remember that most of the people are looking for "hard goods" (antiques or furniture). As people come out of the house, ask them about the goods inside.

3. Make a mental note of who conducts each estate sale you attend. If prices and merchandise were good, then next time you see an ad announcing another sale run by the same people, go to the sale.

4. Map out your territory. Ask where in the house the clothes are located (usually it's in the bedrooms but sometimes clothes are located in several rooms). Go to the clothes first—look at the house later.

5. Make it known to the people conducting the sale that you are interested in clothes. Have them put you on their mailing list for future sales.

6. Bargaining is out until the last hour of the sale. Then go ahead and give it all you've got.

Common clothing finds

- **Look for vintage clothing** from the 20's to the 50's. Clothes are less common at estate sales but usually are of better quality. You will find more women's and men's clothes than children's. Jewelry is also a good buy.

Advantages

- **If you want to save lots of money** on jewelry, a designer dress or a man's suit, you will probably be satisfied.

Disadvantages

- **If you don't like to wait in line,** avoid this type of sale.

Rummage Sales

Rummage sales are almost my favorite clothes shopping sources. It's fun to wait in line outside a church door, not knowing what I will grab when I get inside, but knowing I will find something at a real savings. Last fall I bought my winter coat (a gray, 100% wool, classic-style coat) for $8.00.

One Saturday I found some really terrific bargains at a church rummage sale—without *any* competition! I was late arriving at the church and hurriedly entered the sale area. I scanned the room, planning to start first at the skirts and dresses, and noticed only a few people milling around. This seemed like quite a break, so I proceeded to run from clothes rack to clothes rack, grabbing clothes until my arms were loaded. My heart was racing with excitement as I picked up one great item after another.

Then I heard an announcement over the intercom: "Ladies, we will say a short prayer before we open the doors for the sale." I was stunned and embarrassed to realize the sale hadn't even started. When the prayer was finished, I said sheepishly to a volunteer, "I'm sorry—I didn't know you hadn't started the rummage sale yet." She remarked, "You looked like you really knew what you were doing, so we didn't dare stop you." That was my last opportunity to shop a rummage sale with no other competition! You should also be able to get some fantastic bargains at rummage sales by reading the tips in this section—and you may learn how to beat the competition!

Background

Rummage sales are put on by churches and organizations as fundraisers. They are held in churches, halls, community centers and schools. Once you become acquainted with your local rummage sales, you will find that they will follow a pattern from year to year. These sales can be held on any day of the week but are usually run on weekends.

You'll see rows of tables loaded with clothes at rummage sales, and some sales will have a designer section.

- **How to find one:** look in classified newspaper want ads (*Miscellaneous Sales* or *Household Goods*). Many papers also have a weekly rummage-sale column. Look for posters at the grocery store and notices in church bulletins and school newsletters. Ask your friends when their church or school rummage sales will be held.

Rummage Sale Policies

Savings................95–98% off list—practically free!

Credit............checks with ID (at some), cash

Returns.......................none

Lay-bys.......................none

Bag time.......a time when you can stuff all you can get into a bag for a set price—$1.00 or $2.00—ask about it

Children...........too hectic for pre-schoolers, but great fun for older kids

Common clothing finds

• **Look for current and vintage clothing:** men's suits, shirts and slacks; women's dresses, slacks, sweaters, coats and accessories; and lots of children's clothing. You will often find unique collectors' items in hats and jewelry.

Advantages

• **If you are looking for clothes for a whole family,** a rummage sale can be great because it has an abundance of clothes for everyone. You save a great deal of money. If you are looking for vintage clothes, look here first and save.

Disadvantages

• **If you can't stand crowds and hectic activity,** stay away from rummage sales. A lot of people attend them, so shopping can be very competitive. Since rummage sales aren't held every week, they aren't good clothing sources for people who need something in a hurry.

Tactics for Shopping Rummage Sales

1. Shop with as many people as you can gather together. The more hands grabbing, the more clothes you will all have to choose from.

2. Figure out a method to your rummaging madness before you begin. I start first at the area that is selling what I want most. Then I run to the next priority area. Let your needs determine the pattern.

3. Bring some type of large shopping bag or an empty stroller. This will help free your arms for grabbing more things when you're loaded down with clothes.

4. Get to a sale early for the best buys. You will have to stand in line, but the first people through the door do get the first grab.

5. Grab clothes that appeal to you. Don't stop to think —just literally grab! Don't even bother to check size and condition. When you have grabbed from all the tables and racks (be sure to look under tables too), then go to a corner and start to sort through things to check the fit and condition. Keep alteration possibilities in mind.

6. After you have made your first grab, follow shoppers who are carrying around items that interest you. Tell them pleasantly that you will buy if they don't.

7. Make a final check before you buy. Look in any missed corners, boxes or tables.

8. Bargain! No price at a rummage sale is set in cement.

Garage Sales

If you shop garage sales exclusively for your family's wardrobe, you'll save money and spend a lot of time at it, but you'll have fun doing it. My suggestion for busy people is to combine garage-sale shopping with other bargain sources.

Background

A garage sale (tag sale, yard sale, porch sale, basement sale or apartment sale) is organized by one family or a number of people. They often become social events. You'll find a wide assortment of household goods. Clothes are folded on tables, piled in boxes and hung on make-shift clothes racks.

• **How to find one:** check classified newspaper ads (*Household Goods*, *Miscellaneous Sales*, *Garage* or *Thrift Sales*). Start looking in Wednesday's paper for sales later in the week. Most ads will say whether clothes will be included in the sale. Also, keep an eye out for posters and signs on well-traveled streets. Listen for radio announcements about sales (if you live in a small town).

Garage Sale Policies

Savings...........80–95% off list
Credit.............checks with ID
  (at some), cash
Returns........................none
Lay-bys........................none
Pricing.............bargain if you
  think something is overpriced
Children.........they'll love it—
  and prices fall within their
  budgets!

Common clothing finds

• **Look for women's, children's and men's clothes,** plus shoes and accessories.

• **Look for these good buys:** women's jewelry and accessories, sweaters, sportswear and coats; infants' wear; boys' dress-up clothes, shoes and boots; girls' dresses and everyday play clothes; men's shirts, sweaters and suits.

Advantages

• **If you want to save lots of money,** shop garage sales. Most items are priced to sell. It's hard to believe, but inflation never hit the garage sales! You can almost nickel and dime your way into a wardrobe for the entire family. And if you want to buy household goods too, there are often plenty of great buys.

Disadvantages

• **If you are short on time,** avoid garage sales. This type of wardrobe shopping doesn't offer one-stop convenience. You'll need to shop several garage sales to put together an outfit, and then probably supplement your buys with clothes from other sources. Unless you find this type of shopping recreational, it will definitely be more trouble and seem like work!

• **If you can't resist a bargain,** garage sale prices may trap you into compulsive buying. If that's the case with you, go with a list in hand and stick to it!

Tactics for Shopping Garage Sales

1. Dress casually for the hunt. This will increase your bargaining power. If you plan to try on clothes, wear a leotard or form-fitting clothes under your outfit. You can ask if there's a dressing room, but often there won't be one.

2. Head for multiple-family sales. A good sale will cover a whole block and you can walk from garage to garage.

3. Plan ahead to save a lot on kids' clothes, which are in high demand at garage sales. You can beat this demand by teaming up with others to shop. Invite friends and neighbors to join you. Make a list of sizes and items that everybody's after; then split up and hit as many sales as possible in the first hour.

4. Arrive at a sale earlier than the stated starting time when you are looking for items in great demand. Don't be shy—dealers do this all the time. If you will be out of town or working on the day of a sale, go the night before and explain your circumstances to the person conducting the sale. Ask if you can take a peek at the items you are looking for.

5. Don't be afraid to go slumming. I've gotten some of my best buys from senior citizens whose neighborhoods had changed economically over the last 40 years.

6. Try on anything that catches your eye and looks like it might fit. Sizes can be misleading. Larger sizes may look good belted or altered.

7. Look for out-of-season clothes, because you can really get a bargain on them.

8. Bargain hard (see pages 25–26) in the last few hours of a sale. By this time people are usually ready to get rid of everything. The less they have left over from the sale, the less they have to clean up.

Antique and Vintage Clothing Stores

Many currently popular designers have been inspired by clothing styles of the past. You can duplicate some current fashions by shopping at specialized antique and vintage clothing stores. Or perhaps you're a connoisseur of vintage clothing. If so, you already appreciate the luxurious feel of the silks and rayons of the 20's to the 50's (see pages 144–145).

Background

Antique stores often have a section tucked away for old clothing from the 20's, 30's and sometimes the 40's. It may take a lot of digging to find the clothing section, but it's often worth it! Vintage clothing stores fill a whole store with 30's, 40's and 50's outfits for men and women.

• **How to find one:** look in the yellow pages (*Antiques, Clothing* and *Second-Hand Stores*).

Common clothing finds

• **Antique stores:** look for period clothes dating back to the Victorian era. You may find flapper dresses, satin lingerie, beaded evening purses and better jewelry.

• **Vintage stores:** look for women's beaded 50's sweaters, art deco jewelry, 40's suits, shoes, hats and furs. You'll also find men's sportcoats, silk bathrobes, ties, gabardine trousers, Hawaiian shirts and smoking jackets.

Antique and Vintage Store Policies

Savings ....impossible to say, given inflation, fads, condition of garments, etc.
Credit .....checks with ID, cash
Returns ....none
Lay-bys ....ask about them
Pricing ....garage and rummage sales will be *much* cheaper; the East and West coasts will be more expensive in general

Advantages

• **If you love old movies and styles of the past,** you will have a lot of fun shopping for vintage clothes. You can develop an individual fashion style.

Disadvantages

• **If you don't have an interest in old clothes,** don't bother with this type of shopping. In the past few years, vintage clothing has become very popular and expensive.

Tactics for Shopping Antique and Vintage Stores

1. Check vintage clothes carefully for stress points (see pages 98–99). Stains can be a problem to remove (remember these clothes are old—so the fabric may be fragile and the stains have been sitting for a long time).

2. Try on clothes you like, no matter what the size (this applies to both men and women).

3. Ask the shopkeeper for help when you are looking for a specific item. It may be kept in the back or may be expected in a new shipment. Ask to be called when it comes in.

4. Ask the shopkeeper to recommend a drycleaner who's experienced with vintage clothing. Most of the old fabrics do need to be professionally cleaned.

5. Bargain! You can point out a flaw, but most of the clothes will have flaws due to age. Just ask, "How much would you be willing to come down?"

Government Surplus Stores

Fashion designers in the last decade have reproduced a style that started as a 60's college campus trend—the "military look" in clothing (jump suits, fatigue pants, leather bomber jackets). If this is your style, there's a way to beat department store prices and civilian-manufactured clothing construction.

All government-issued uniform gear is rigorously tested for durability and wearability in design and fabric. Take advantage of this expertise and buy high-quality military clothing at civilian prices in government surplus stores. You'll be right in style!

Background

A government surplus or military surplus store sells a variety of military goods, from clothing to tents. You will find clothes from the United States military, the British military, the French Foreign Legion and other military groups around the world. Items can be new or second-hand from previous wars. The store owner gets merchandise by bidding on government surplus stock.

• **How to find one:** check the yellow pages (*Surplus Stores*).

Common clothing finds

• **Look for heavy-duty clothing:** field jackets, military trench coats, all-wool uniform shirts and slacks, fatigue pants, navy pea coats, World War II bomber jackets, cotton long-johns, flight suits and ammunition packs. All of the merchandise will be made with quality construction features: sturdy sewing, heavy zippers, durable buttons. You will find tightly woven fabric in wool, cotton, silk and gabardine.

Government Surplus Store Policies

Savings...............50–75% off civilian military-designed clothes at list prices
Credit.........bank credit cards (at some), checks with ID (at some), cash
Returns...............frowned on but worth a try if you find a problem
Lay-bys.........ask about them

Advantages

• **If you have a creative sense** for putting together an outfit, you will want to add surplus shopping to your list. Most stores don't bother with imaginative displays, so it's up to you to invent looks. But you'll save money and end up with a unique look wearing well-made clothing.

• **If you're looking for durable clothing,** perhaps to wear as work clothes for yard work or hiking clothes, you'll be able to find long-lasting, well-made items here. And the prices will be much lower than at a store that specializes in clothing for outdoor recreation!

Disadvantages

• **If you want a specific item quickly,** surplus store shopping may not fit the bill. Sizes are often large for women and the range is spotty. Stock can be erratic: there could be racks and racks of military trench coats and a few British navy sweaters or just the opposite. It really depends on what the store bids for and purchases.

Tactics for Shopping Government Surplus Stores

1. Make sure you are really shopping in a government surplus store with military regulation clothing. Some stores advertise "military style" clothing, but these clothes don't have the same quality construction or fabric. Ask the store owner where the stock comes from.

2. If you have more than one store in your area and you are looking for a specific item, phone the stores and do some comparison-pricing. Prices will vary from store to store.

3. Choose military classics that have become civilian classics—for example, navy pea coats, military trench coats, Eisenhower jackets, field jackets and jackets with hoods hidden in zippered collars. Both olive drab and camouflage can be fashionable if you handle them right. But don't get swept away by the good prices and values and end up looking like you're AWOL!

4. Men might start by looking in a size category that's smaller than usual. Women may have to try on a lot of clothes before finding the proper fit.

5. If you find something great, don't hesitate—buy. It may not be there the second time around. But don't jump at something that's not in good condition. Hold out, and something better will come along.

Funky Functional Clothing Stores

Some vintage clothing stores fit this category, but if you find a second-hand store near a college campus or artsy neighborhood it will probably harbor more funky functional clothing than vintage clothes.

The Canal Jean Company and the Unique Clothing Warehouse in the Soho district of Manhattan are examples of stores that sell chic new and second-hand clothes. Punk rock music blares while you shop. In many stores you will find brightly tinted outfits hanging in avant-garde fashion on the walls and some of the customers' hair will be dyed the same colors as the clothing (purple, orange or pink)!

Background

This type of store bids on and buys large quantities of new and used clothing from many sources: the military, manufacturers' close-outs, even professional rag-pickers around the world. The clothes are cleaned and sorted at a main warehouse and the styles in high demand are displayed in the stores en masse. Clothes are sold out of bins and bunched together on racks, and the turnover is fast. These stores are *not* run by charitable organizations; they are profit-making ventures.

• **How to find one:** look in the yellow pages (*Second-Hand Stores*).

Common clothing finds

• **Casual, chic clothes:** look for jeans, painters' pants, military gear, vintage clothing and bins of sweaters, slacks and dresses.

Advantages

• **If you have fun putting together unusual outfits,** you will love a funky functional clothing store. It's a cheap way to put together your own personal look.

Disadvantages

• **If you prefer a traditional, classic style,** this type of store is not for you. It's "cheap chic" shopping. However, if you are looking for some of the military classics (pea coats or trench coats), this type of store sometimes sells military gear for less than the government surplus stores.

Funky Functional Store Policies

Savings...........65–90% off list
Credit........bank credit cards, checks with ID, cash
Returns.......................none
Lay-bys.........ask about them

Flea Markets

If you like to people-watch in large crowds and shop while you're doing it, go to a flea market (also known as a swap meet, especially in the Southwest). There's an overwhelming variety of merchan-

Tactics for Shopping Funky Functional Clothing Stores

1. Shop when your energy is high and your time is ample. You may find just what you want, finally, at the bottom of a bin after an hour of sifting.

2. Shop during the week, as these stores are packed with college and high-school students on Saturdays.

3. Take a glance at the store's fashion displays to help you put together a funky outfit.

4. Try on any clothes that command your interest. Sizes are often erratic.

5. Check the clothing carefully for flaws, stains and any other irregularities.

6. Remember that bargaining is minimal.

dise and all the hustle, pitch and bargaining is reminiscent of the thieves' market in Mexico City or of famous flea markets in Europe. It's a great way to spend a Sunday afternoon.

Background

Flea markets are rather like country fairs; they are usually held in large parking lots or buildings on weekends. People bring their goods to sell and set up shop at tables. You will find row after row of vendors who have rented their space by the day and either do this as a sideline to other jobs or as part of their business. Some are antique dealers, some garbage haulers, others private parties trying to sell their wares. For some, selling large items such as stoves or washing machines is easier at a flea market than at a garage sale.

- **How to find one:** look in the classified ads in your newspaper (*Miscellaneous Sales*). Some flea markets run an ad each weekend. Watch for signs in the supermarket and along well-traveled streets. Also phone the chamber of commerce in your area and ask for flea market locations.

Flea Market Policies

Savings...............20–65%—it depends on the goods and your bargaining ability
Credit.............checks with ID (sometimes), cash—go with cash
Returns........................none
Lay-bys........................none
Pricing....................bargain! If you want something, finger it, admire it, hesitate, then start to walk away—that'll start the haggling!

Common clothing finds

- **Look for everything** from work clothes to jewelry to infants' clothes. The merchandise is new and second-hand, with some antiques. The type of items you will find varies from weekend to weekend.

Advantages

- **If you like the Old World flavor of open markets,** this will be fun for you. You can browse, talk with people and pick through all types of items.

Children love it. It's definitely entertaining, and you do sometimes get a good deal, especially if you really know prices and quality in the items you need.

Disadvantages

- **If you're short on time,** skip flea markets. This is entertainment shopping, even though it can lead to great savings.

- **If you are a naturally suspicious person,** you may feel like the seller is trying to put something over on you. That may be partly true, and it could happen if you are not familiar with the going price on the items you want.

- **If you can't resist buying** in a market atmosphere, you could lose money at a flea market.

Tactics for Shopping Flea Markets

1. You must take your merchandise home with you when you buy it, so come prepared with something to get it home in.

2. Wear a leotard or tight-fitting clothes that you can put other clothing over. There won't be dressing rooms.

3. Be careful when buying expensive jewelry unless you really know your stuff. Sometimes a seller exaggerates the quality of a gem.

4. Bargain aggressively toward the end of a day. Most sellers have to pack up whatever's left and tote it home, so they are usually happy to sell rather than pack.

Auctions

Auctions are of great interest to antique collectors and second-hand furniture seekers, but the buyer who is only looking for clothes will find auctions a limited shopping market. However, if you want to combine fun with purchasing clothes *and* furniture, you will find an auction a good bargain source.

Background

Auctions are conducted by an auctioneer who oversees and generates bidding within the auction crowd. The merchandise may come from the estate of someone who has passed away, or from a family who is moving, or from private sellers who want to make some money. Auctions are held on weekday evenings or on weekends. Most are conducted at auction firms nowadays, though some are still held right in the home, farmhouse or barn of the owner of the goods to be sold.

• **How to find one:** look in the classified ads of your newspaper (*Miscellaneous Sales* or *Antiques*). Most auction firms run a weekly ad. Check the yellow pages (*Auctioneers*). Phone the auctioneers and ask when and where their next auction will be held. Also, ask if you can get on a mailing list for notices of upcoming sales.

Common clothing finds

• **Expect to find older clothing**—vintage items from

Auction Policies

Savings...........40–65% off list
Credit........................cash or certified checks, unless you know the auctioneer
Returns.......................none
Lay-bys.......................none
Bidding ....methods vary—raising your hand, nodding or waving a paddle you're given—so ask beforehand
Other policies.......should be printed in the sale catalog or posted at the sale. Know them for your own good.

---

the 30's, 40's and 50's. Sometimes you'll see furs, and often you'll see jewelry (the more expensive costume jewelry: gold, silver and semi-precious stones). When you phone about an auction, ask the auctioneer what types of clothing will be featured.

Advantages

• **If you want more than just clothing** or if you are interested in jewelry, an auction can be a very entertaining way to shop. You will be bidding against some dealers, but if you win the bid, you will save.

Disadvantages

• **If you're just buying clothes,** an auction will be too limited and time-consuming to warrant the money you save. You may also catch auction-buying fever and bid for something you don't really need.

Tactics for Shopping Auctions

1. If you feel unsure about buying at an auction and wish you had more experience, it helps to attend an auction and just observe things once. You'll get your feet wet and learn a lot by watching other people. Sit in the back.

2. Go early for the inspection time. Each auction will have a time for you to preview the items. Make a thorough check of the articles you want to buy.

3. Keep a disinterested posture when you're inspecting the merchandise at the preview and once you start bidding. A poker face is essential. Any excited interest could push up the price.

4. If the auctioneer has to decide a draw, more often than not it will be decided in favor of the person sitting nearest the front.

5. Set a firm price limit and stick to it! Don't go over that amount when you bid.

6. Don't bid on an item you haven't inspected beforehand. You may be disappointed later by the size, color or condition of the item. Once you win the bid, the item is yours.

Post Office Auctions

Post office auctions are fun, fast-moving and full of all kinds of merchandise. If you live near one of the dead parcel branch locations of the U.S. Post Office (see page 119), attend at least one—it's an exciting experience.

One woman I know bought a mink stole for $125.00 at one of the auctions. Before she left the Post Office, she was offered $200.00 for the stole by a dealer. She refused the offer—the mink was later appraised at $1,000.00.

Background

Any goods that are lost or damaged through the mail make their way to one of the Post Office's 19 dead parcel branches in the United States. Approximately eight times a year, these branches have public auctions. You can inspect the merchandise for one hour before the auction begins. The auction takes about two hours. All the items are sold by the box, bin or barrel. These are all numbered, so when the bidding starts you bid on the numbered bin you want. If you win, you've got to take *all* the goods in the bin, even if you're only after one thing.

• **How to find one:** phone the Post Office dead parcel branches near you (see page 119). Ask when the next auction will be held.

Common finds

• **Look for a variety of merchandise:** clothes, jewelry, furs, books, dishes, antiques, electronic equipment. Sometimes the Post Office also sells government surplus items. It's unpredictable shopping—in one barrel of clothing inspected at an auction, I found a silk sarong with matching alligator sandals . . . the whole barrel sold for $40.00.

Advantages

• **If you have friends who want to join you** and split a bin of clothes or merchandise, you can have a good time and save money doing it. It's fun later when you rummage through all the crazy items you end up with.

Disadvantages

• **If you are looking for a specific item,** this type of shopping will be too unpredictable for you. You may want only one item in a bin, but unless you split a bin with a friend you will be stuck with everything.

• **If the contents of a bin turn out to be useless** to you, you're stuck with the job of getting rid of it. Don't forget to get tax deductions if you donate your rejects to charitable groups.

Post Office Auction Policies

Savings...........50–85% off list (varies)

Credit............checks with ID, cash (you may need the check ok'd before the auction)

Returns.....none—everything is "as is"

Lay-bys.......................none

Announcements.......get on the P.O. mailing list to get the catalog of merchandise a week before the sale

Bidding...........very informal; minimum bids are $1.00

Post Office Dead Parcel Branches

The dead parcel branches are located at the main Post Office in the following cities.

Atlanta, Georgia
Bell, California
Boston, Massachusetts
Chicago, Illinois
Cincinnati, Ohio
Denver, Colorado
Detroit, Michigan
Fort Worth, Texas
Greensboro, North Carolina
Jacksonville, Florida
Memphis, Tennessee
New York, New York
Philadelphia, Pennsylvania
Pittsburgh, Pennsylvania
St. Louis, Missouri
St. Paul, Minnesota
San Francisco, California
Seattle, Washington
Washington, D.C.

Tactics for Shopping Post Office Auctions

1. Examine your catalog when you receive it. Do some price investigating on the articles you want to buy before the day of the auction. This will help you determine how much you are willing to bid.

2. Inspect the items beforehand and determine what you want to buy and how high you will go on your bid. Then stick to it. Be careful of "auction fever"—don't get carried away and bid on something you don't really want.

3. Bring several people with you to the auction and split a bin to cut costs further.

4. Bring your own boxes or bags to carry home the merchandise you buy.

Unusual Clothing Sources

If you're new to second-hand clothes shopping, I'm sure many of the sources you've read about in this chapter have been surprising to you. But I want to give even veteran bargain hunters a few new leads, so here goes!

Drycleaners

Most drycleaners have unclaimed clothes they leave in storage for months or years before they donate them to charitable organizations. See if you can find a friendly drycleaner in your area who will let you dig through all the forgotten apparel. I've done it for years at my relatives' cleaning business, finding gorgeous wedding gowns, formals, men's tuxedos and everyday clothes.

• **Don't be shy**—you may be doing the cleaner a favor. He or she can only receive a tax credit on the cost of the cleaning, not on the value of the garment.

• **Know your prices.** I suggest you "shop" this source after you have a firm knowledge of second-hand clothing prices. The cleaners will not know what to charge, so you must be prepared to make them an offer.

Garbage haulers

There are many garbage haulers who, by virtue of their profession, become collectors of antiques and all sorts of unique items. Some of them sell these items on weekends at flea markets.

Clothing is often simply discarded in the garbage, especially when a family member passes away. If you are interested in vintage clothing, a garbage hauler can be a good contact for you.

• **Call a few** and give them your name and number. Tell them you would be interested in buying old clothes.

• **Be prepared.** You will have to make an offer, so know the current price and don't pay a lot.

Maintenance, Updates, Repairs and Alterations

Fashion experts claim that a practical, long-lasting wardrobe is a combination of some new styles every season along with the accumulation of classic basics. This allows you to add new looks to your wardrobe without completely revamping it each year. If you follow this approach to outfitting your closet, maintenance, updates and repairs will be major aids in keeping control over your clothing costs. The way you take care of your clothes will help determine how long your wardrobe will last—and how much money you'll need to spend on new clothes. Time you spend on simple everyday care can save you money in replacement costs and drycleaning bills. Clothes do respond to care, so invest a little in them to save a lot.

Extending your clothes' life

1. Cut down on wear. If your working clothes are expensive, change to others when you don't need to wear them.

2. Check clothes for spots or stains after each wearing. Use a stain remover immediately. The longer stains remain in fabric, the harder they are to remove.

3. Remove bulky objects from jacket and pants pockets.

4. Brush clothes to remove crumbs and surface dirt. It's easier to do this while the clothes are hanging.

5. Put clothes away properly. Fold knits. Hang blouses, dresses, skirts, jackets and coats. This will help retain the garment's shape.

6. Don't hang clothes on bare wire hangers—use plastic, wooden or foam-padded wire ones.

7. Let your clothes rest and reshape (this also goes for shoes). Give them a day off between wearings.

8. Make small sewing repairs as soon as possible (buttons, hem rips and so on).

9. Wear arm shields to protect delicate fabrics from perspiration stains.

10. Use a spray-on stain repellent on men's ties, fabric purses and fabric shoes.

11. Dryclean a whole suit, not just the slacks. This will prevent mismatched pieces. Also point out stains to the drycleaner. It helps them to treat the stain.

12. Don't have garments cleaned any more than necessary, since cleaning may wear down the fabric.

Extending your shoes' life

1. **Brush suede shoes** or boots after each wear. If you live in a wet climate, spray them with a water repellent.

2. **Polish leather shoes** and boots when they are new to help prevent scuffing.

3. **Let mud dry** on shoes before brushing it off. Stuff wet shoes with newspapers and keep them away from heat.

4. **Saddlesoap leather** to remove surface dirt; then

polish and buff for a high gloss.

5. **Use a shoe tree,** not your closet floor, for storage. Or punch holes in a cardboard shoe box. Don't use plastic shoe boxes, because leather needs to air out.

6. **Clean synthetic shoes** with household spray or window cleaner.

7. **Don't use liquid shoe polish on leather,** because it may dry the leather out.

8. **Don't let shoes wear down** completely before you try to repair them (see page 127).

Handy basics for clothing and shoe care

☐ A good clothes brush

☐ A suede brush (stiff bristle)

☐ Art gum erasers, emery boards or fine sandpaper to remove scuff marks from suede

☐ Soil repellent spray

☐ Water repellent spray for suede

☐ Stain remover (look for one of the easy-to-use stain pens)

☐ Spray-on sizing for ironing

☐ Cold-water soap for gentle fabrics and woolens

☐ Presoaks for tough stains, laundry detergent, fabric softener

☐ Sewing kit: thread, needle, pins, tape measure, scissors

☐ Saddle soap for leather shoes, belts and purses

☐ Shoe polish (wax type), shoe brush and soft cloth

Updating Your Wardrobe

If you have a garment that's made of quality fabric (see pages 30–34), consider the following update possibilities. Often fabrics outlive the fashion life of the garments they are in. Today, since pure natural fabrics such as wools and linens are very costly to replace, updating your wardrobe can save you money even when you pay someone else to do the job.

Updating jackets

Jackets are simply too expensive to retire from your closet without a fight. Here are a few alteration and style suggestions that will help you get the most wear out of dated jackets.

• **Shoulders and chest:** most renovation in this part of a jacket is a major tailoring job. However, it's worth it if the jacket is of quality fabric, in good condition and a pivotal point in your wardrobe.

• **Lapels:** lapels can always be slimmed down and reshaped. But unless you're an experienced seamstress, don't try it yourself. Let a professional do it.

• **Waistline:** tapering the torso (see Figure 1) works well on heavy coats and men's suit

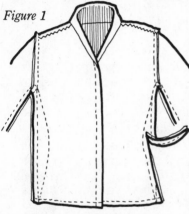

Figure 1

Tapering the torso

Figure 2

Taking in darts

jackets. This method can also be used on blazers, blouses and dresses. Taking darts in on the front (see Figure 2) works well on blazers, blouses and straight dresses. Try on the garment to see where the bustline falls. Mark the top point of the bust and the top of the hip, decide how much fullness you want taken out in the middle area, and pin. Make sure the darts on both sides of the garment match and are centered properly.

• **Jacket length:** shortening works best on a simply designed jacket. It's easier to alter a jacket that's not fully lined. To see how the jacket proportion will change, try standing in front of a full-length mirror. Use a few straight pins and experiment with the length. If the jacket begins to look more current and is still flattering to your body shape, have it altered.

• **Style:** if the lapels are only slightly too wide for the current fashion and the fabric is dark, don't bother with alterations. Wear the jacket with a brightly colored shirt or blouse. Eyes will be drawn away from the lapel area. Also, your fashion sense will help you change the look of a jacket with accessories (see page 149). Consider changing or adding buttons or a belt to make a jacket jump back into fashion.

Updating slacks

It's a simple update to narrow your wide-legged pants. This works well on unlined slacks with a basic straight seam. Don't give up a good pair of slacks before you've checked these tips.

• **Width:** see Figure 3. Turn your unlined slacks inside out. Rip out the hems. Lay the slacks on an ironing board and use a yardstick to help keep a straight line. Mark and pin the desired width equally off both the inside and outside seams up to the crotch (most narrow slacks are 18 or 20 inches around; 16 inches is skinny). Machine stitch down the seams. Cut off the excess material with a pinking shear to avoid unraveling. Rehem the slacks.

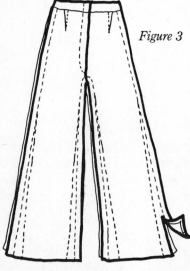

Figure 3

Narrowing the width of slacks

• **Length:** if there's a cuff on a pant, you can easily add approximately 1½ inches in length to your slacks. Snip the threads where the cuff is tacked to the seams. Then press out the crease. This works well on most fabrics except for silk, velvet, corduroy or polyester. These fabrics will leave permanent creases at the hem.

• **Size:** don't bother to cut down more than one size, unless the pants are very expensive to replace.

• **Style:** if the fashion magazines are showing pants tucked into boots, try it using old slacks that are too wide or too short. Or if culottes are being shown over boots, cut off a pair of outdated slacks and hem them to the current vogue length.

Updating skirts

• **Length:** long wool holiday skirts are sometimes put to better use when shortened to a daytime length. Also remember this when buying second-hand (see page 131).

• **Width:** see Figure 4. Take an A-line skirt and make it into a straight skirt. Lay the A-line skirt flat, place a straight skirt on top and use it as a pattern. Pin down the sides of the A-line skirt, following the width of the straight skirt. Turn the skirt inside out and machine stitch along your pin line; then clip the excess. If the skirt has a seam in the front, back or side, choose one and open the seam as a kick pleat.

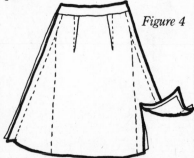

Figure 4

Narrowing the width of skirts

• **Style:** often simply changing how you wear a sweater or blouse with a skirt will make an update difference.

Updating shirts

The collar is the main area of a shirt that may need updating. Making a long, pointy collar into a small, rounded one is tricky for beginning seamstresses but can be done by advanced seamstresses. They can also "turn" worn collars on men's shirts (removing them from the neckband and reversing them so the wear is concealed) for under $5.00. Or consider removing a collar altogether if it's outmoded. Both are inexpensive alterations if you take them to a seamstress, and they just may do the trick in prolonging the life of a quality 100% cotton shirt.

• **Size:** you can taper a shirt in the same way as shown on page 123. For men's shirts, use Figure 1.

• **Collars:** see Figure 5. To shorten a long shirt collar into a small collar, follow these directions. The following method works well on a man's type shirt that has the extra collar piece (a neckband). Remove the top collar piece. Turn it inside out. Pin the collar width to measure the same distance all the way around (use the back of the collar's maximum width as your measurement). Machine stitch on the inside along pins. Cut off the excess fabric. Turn the collar right side out and press. Top stitch the collar and sew it back onto the shirt.

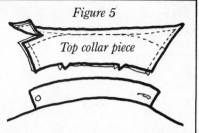

Figure 5

Top collar piece

Shortening a shirt collar

• **Style:** always try belting a favorite shirt, tying it at the waist or folding up the cuffs to give it a smart fashion look.

Updating men's ties

• **Narrowing:** if you have a favorite silk tie that's now too wide, have it narrowed by a tailor or seamstress. This should be an inexpensive alteration.

Updating kids' clothes

• **Holes:** to cover holes and stains on children's clothes, it's easy to add an iron-on patch or applique.

• **Length:** if you're adding length to little girls' clothes and there's a permanent crease left from the old hemline, cover this by adding a rick-rack trim.

• **Recycling:** if you are an experienced seamstress, you can cut up adult clothing and use it as fabric for making children's garments.

• **Other ideas:** take a look at the recycling clothes guide to help give you some ideas (see page 131). You may also want to consider these recycling tips when you're buying second-hand adult clothes and you see fabric in excellent condition.

Repairing Your Clothes

Tailors and drycleaners have camouflaged the wear on men's suits and shirts for years. Such professional mending or mending you do yourself may save you from expensive replacement costs. If a damaged or worn garment is expensive and made of costly fabric (leather, suede, fur, wool) or is part of a suit or ensemble, you will want to try to redeem it. Also, when you examine second-hand clothing, you need to judge whether an item will be a good buy, including any wear or repair costs. Read through the following tips and determine whether you can repair the damage yourself or should call in an expert. If you prefer to make your own repairs, one helpful book is *Mend It*, by Maureen Goldsworthy.

Simple repairs

These repairs are small jobs of the type that an inexperienced seamstress could easily perform.

- **Covering up:** to camouflage wear on women's and girls' clothes, use iron-on patches, sew on your own patches (good for boys), or sew on trim or appliques. You can also move the back pockets to patch holes in the knees.

- **Seaming out a tear or wear:** on generously cut garments, you may be able to position a dart or seam to "seam out" the problem.

- **Closing holes:** on split seams, restitch on the wrong side, along the existing seam.

- **Closing rips:** try to glue together the rips in torn vinyl, leather and some fabric garments.

- **Lengthening:** add extra fabric for length to little girls' dresses.

- **Keeping closed:** add on or move buttons.

Average repairs

These repairs are slightly more difficult, but the average seamstress should have no trouble with them.

- **Replacing parts:** replace the panel of a garment when you have leftover fabric. This works well on men's suit pants in the seat area. The material doesn't have to match perfectly if the suit jacket is worn all the time.

- **Patching wear:** add leather or suede patches to jacket elbows. You can also add this fabric or fabric binding to worn jacket cuffs and the front of jacket openings.

- **Hiding wear:** turn under torn shirt collars and cuffs.

- **Renewing edges:** repair worn buttonholes and pocket edges.

- **Renewing closings:** replace broken zippers.

Difficult repairs

Only an experienced seamstress should attempt to do these repairs.

- **Camouflaging:** reweave or darn a cigarette burn or hole that is not in the seam.

- **Remaking:** reline a man's suit coat or sportcoat. Also reline heavy outerwear.

- **Replacing:** replace panels on leather or suede garments.

Repairing and Restyling Shoes

If you've shopped for a good pair of shoes lately, you know how much the prices have increased. It's not unusual to spend $70.00 on a pair of quality pumps or $40.00 for athletic shoes. An alternative to paying the high cost of new shoes may be in saving the pair in your closet. But refurbishing a pair of shoes is not necessarily cheap. Don't do it if the shoes are badly worn in the uppers and insoles. You have waited too long.

To determine whether your shoes are worth a fix-up, ask yourself these two questions: Would the shoes be expensive to replace? Is the shoe design classic enough to wear for several seasons? If the answers are yes, go ahead.

Find a good shoe-repair person. Ask for a recommendation from friends, your drycleaner or a salesperson at a better shoe store. Go to a shop that not only repairs, but can also restyle shoes. Here are a few services you may want to consider.

Repairs

- **Replacing heels and heel lifts:** when 20% of a flat-type heel is worn down or 50% of a woman's high-heel lift is gone, it's time for a repair. These repairs cost from $3.00 to $9.00 for men's shoes, and from $2.00 to $4.00 for women's heel lifts (see Figures 6 and 7). Note that if the worn area goes past the lift on a women's shoe into the high heel, it will be a more expensive repair.

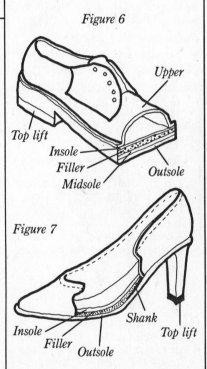

Figure 6

Upper

Top lift

Insole

Filler

Midsole

Outsole

Figure 7

Shank

Insole

Filler

Outsole

Top lift

- **Resoling regular shoes:** a new half-sole will usually do the job on most shoes. A good repair person can resole your shoes four or five times. Men's shoes can be done for $9.00 to $15.00; women's shoes, from $8.00 to $11.00. It's very important to bring your shoe to a competent repair person. Bad workmanship can distort the width of the shoe.

• **Resoling special shoes:** tennis and running shoes can be resoled for a cost of $12.00 to $20.00. Crepe soles can be replaced for $10.00 to $18.00.

Restyling

• **Heels:** you can totally change the style of a heel or take up to an inch off a woman's high heel for a new style.

• **Toes:** open the toes on a pair of shoes, or have a pump trans-

formed into a slingback style.

Other shoe repair services

Think twice before you write off your footwear—reinvesting in it may prolong its life considerably for very little cost.

• **Dyeing:** you can have both cloth and leather shoes dyed.

• **Removing squeaks.**

• **Stretching** to fit.

• **Replacing zippers** on leather goods.

Quick Tricks for Clothes Maintenance, Updates and Repairs

Spend half an hour in a notions department or fabric store and you'll find some quick aids for changing, maintaining and repairing your wardrobe. These are especially helpful for non-seamstresses.

☐ Stitch Witchery—a product that lets you iron up hems rather than sew them.

☐ Iron-on patches. You can also make your own iron-ons with fabric, by using large squares of Stitch Witchery.

☐ Fabric adhesives for leather, vinyl and cloth.

☐ Iron-on initials for blouses, men's shirts and blazers.

☐ Glue-on velcro fasteners.

☐ Iron-on replacements for pockets.

☐ Instant coloring for leather and vinyl shoes, handbags or belts.

☐ Quick shoeshine packets. (These are great when you're traveling.)

☐ Shoe trees for storing shoes.

☐ Shoe laces for all types of shoes.

☐ Shoe cushion insoles and heel liners for shoes that don't fit properly.

☐ Padded hangers for delicate fabrics and furs.

☐ Collar stays for men's and women's shirts.

☐ Dress shields to prevent perspiration stains.

☐ Iron-on shoulder pads.

☐ Washable markers you can use when making wardrobe alterations.

☐ Ready-made rib-knit collars to be sewn on polo shirts.

☐ Stain removers and delicate fabric detergent.

☐ Ribbons (great for tying at necks of blouses), fabric trim and appliques for covering wear on clothes.

Choosing an Alteration Expert

Knowing a good alteration specialist is a real asset to your wardrobe—and to your budget. Stylish alterations will extend your clothes' life, fashionably, for a nominal investment. If you don't sew yourself, an alteration expert is essential when you're buying second-hand clothes. You can take advantage of huge savings when you alter someone else's wardrobe to fit you! Simple alterations can certainly be done by anyone who sews (see pages 122–125). But bring more complicated overhauls to a tailor or seamstress, preferably one who also does custom designed clothes. These people seem to have a good flair for fashion.

Finding a specialist

• **Ask fussy, fashionable acquaintances** who alters their clothes. In any service business a good referral usually means good quality work.

• **Call a school** in your area that teaches fabric and design. This can sometimes produce a very enthusiastic and reasonable alteration person. Try the local university or vocational school.

• **Watch the ads** in local newspapers (and check the classified section of larger circulation papers) for notices of other professionals. When you call, follow the tips below to check out their credentials. Also ask for the names and phone numbers of a few customers so you can check on their performance.

Checking a specialist out

• **Ask to see a list of services** when you go into an alterations shop. The more the shop can offer you, the better. This will save you transportation time.

• **Find out how expert the person is.** You may be willing to spend more money on alterations that are superbly done— the excellent work may be worth the cost. How long has he or she been doing this type of work? Does the expert specialize in women's or men's clothes? Ask if the alteration expert will redo, at no extra charge, any garment that doesn't fit properly when the job is completed.

• **Ask about drycleaning.** If you bring your clothes to a tailor who sends any necessary drycleaning out to another expert, it's costing you more money. You are better off bringing it to your own drycleaner for the cleaning work.

• **On the other hand,** if you bring your clothes to a drycleaner to be altered or tailored, it may take longer than you want to wait. The first priority is to get the cleaning done; alterations come second. Ask how long it will take. Also be sure that your cleaner does not have to send your job out to a tailor; you're sure to save money if you take the work to a tailor yourself.

Alteration Rating Scale

This chart rates a wide variety of alterations by their relative difficulty. Remember that it's always easier to make something smaller than to make it larger. And don't ever try to make an alteration if it will cost more than half of the garment's value or if you don't foresee a lot of wear from it when altered.

	Minor	Average	Difficult	Major	No Way
Coats	Moving buttons over for fit.	Hemming. Shortening sleeves.	Tapering waist and sleeves.	Enlarging arm holes. Narrowing shoulders.	Widening shoulders.
Blazers	Same as above.	Hemming. Narrowing waist.	Narrowing lapels.	Relining a man's sportcoat or suit jacket.	Widening shoulders.
Slacks (Men's pants are easier to alter than women's pants.)	Taking in the waistline when there's no waistband.	Tapering legs.	Taking in waist when there's a waistband.	Raising the crotch area.	
Skirts	Hemming.	Changing an A-line skirt to a straight skirt.	Hemming and pressing an accordion pleat skirt.		
Shirts	Tapering width. Shortening sleeve length.	Making collars smaller.			

Recycling Clothes

You can sometimes make a garment work in an additional or new way, once it's lived its original life. Use this guide to help you change men's and women's clothes into new garments for women and children. These ideas can boost your imagination. You may find new ways to recycle old favorites.

	Recycled for Women	Recycled for Children
Shirts	Turn a flannel shirt into a vest. Velour shirts make nice vests.	Men's heavy workshirts can be made into a pair of pants. Dresses can be made from large T-shirts.
Dresses	Make into tunic tops, a blouse or a skirt.	A woman's dress can be turned into a child's dress.
Skirts	Turn a full skirt into a cape.	A woman's long skirt can be turned into a child's dress, skirt or pants.
Slacks	Cut off legs for shorts or culottes.	Make jeans or corduroys into a little girl's skirt. Make a vest.
Sweaters	Make a vest.	Make a vest.
Blazers	Take the sleeves off for a vest.	Turn blazers into vests.
Coats	Make a shorter version, ¾ length or a jacket.	Transform an adult's coat into a winter vest.
Snowsuits		Cut off an adult's snowsuit and make it into a jacket.

Typical Alteration Charges for Women's Clothes

The following figures will give you a ballpark idea of typical alteration costs. Compared to prices charged in locations all over the U.S.
and Canada, these prices are medium to high. Use this chart as a
guide, but check several services around your area to get the best
price available.

Blazers and Suit Jackets

Narrowing lapels $35.00
Narrowing shoulders $35.00
Body tapering:
    with side seams . . . . $ 8.00
    plus center vent $12.00
Shortening length $12.00
Shortening sleeves . . . . $ 8.00

Slacks

Narrowing legs:
    single seam . . . . $ 9.00
    double seam (jeans) $12.50
Hemming . . . . $ 3.75
Hemming and cuffing . . . . $ 5.50
Taking in waist . . . . $ 4.00

Coats

Narrowing lapels $35.00
Narrowing shoulders $35.00
Body tapering:
    with side seams $10.00
    plus center vent $15.00
Shortening length $20.00
Shortening sleeves . . . . $ 8.00

Dresses and Skirts

Hemming . . . . $ 6.00
Narrowing width . . . . $ 9.00

Blouses

Narrowing collars . . . . $ 7.00
Tapering body . . . . $ 4.00
Shortening sleeves . . . . $ 5.00

Typical Alteration Charges for Men's Clothes

The following figures will give you a ballpark idea of typical alteration costs. Compared to prices charged in locations all over the U.S.
and Canada, these prices are medium to high. Use this chart as a
guide, but check several services around your area to get the best
price available.

Sportcoats, Blazers and Suit Jackets

Narrowing lapels $35.00
Narrowing shoulders $40.00
Body tapering:
   with side seams................$10.00
   plus center vent................$15.00
Shortening length.................$15.00
Shortening sleeves ....$ 8.00

Trousers

Hemming ....$ 4.00
Hemming and cuffing.............$ 5.50
Narrowing legs $10.50
Taking in waist...................$ 5.00

Coats

Narrowing lapels $35.00
Narrowing shoulders $40.00
Body tapering:
   with side seams................$15.00
   plus center vent................$20.00
Shortening length.................$20.00
Shortening sleeves ....$ 8.00

Shirts

Tapering body ....$ 5.00
Narrowing collars................$ 8.00 to $10.00
Turning collars..................$ 3.50 to $ 5.00
Shortening sleeves ....$ 5.50

Ties

Narrowing ties ....$ 5.00 to $12.00

Leather Maintenance

You can prolong the life of a beat-up grain leather coat by four or five years with professional cleaning and dyeing. Suede can also be revived, but not as easily. Thus leather serves as a better investment material than suede for most garments. According to Don Poach, an expert leather cleaner in Minneapolis, "It's the cheapest garment to maintain."

Maintaining your leather's life

• **Save care labels and hang tags** when you buy leather. Later these will be very helpful to a leather cleaner.

• **Keep it clean.** Wipe grain leather with mild soap and lukewarm water. Let dry and buff with a soft cloth.

• **Iron carefully.** When you press leather garments, put heavy brown paper between the iron and the material. Move the iron constantly to avoid hot spots. Don't use steam.

• **Don't store leather in plastic bags.** It needs air circulation to keep from drying out. Store in a cool closet.

Reclaiming your leather's life

Cleaning leather or suede demands a special process. This process preserves the finish and color of your garment. Cleaning once a year is sufficient.

• **Take your garment to a specialist** in cleaning leather or suede. Find one by looking in the yellow pages under *Leather and Suede Cleaning*. If you take your garment to a drycleaner, who in turn must send it to the expert, it will usually cost you more time and money. Most leather cleaners prefer to work directly with their customers, because then the customers are available for questions.

Dyeing leather

When a leather garment is being made, the skins are immersed in dye (vat-dyed) and then sewn together. Later, when you want a garment re-dyed, only the surface can be colored. This makes it difficult to dye a garment a different color, even a darker one, because as dye wears off the original color will show through. For this reason, most good leather dyers encourage you to stay in the same color family if you want to dye leather goods.

• **Know the type of leather** you buy and ask what the dyeing possibilities are for the leather. If you are buying from a reputable dealer, you can expect answers to your questions.

• **Find an expert.** A leather cleaner is also a leather dyer. Look in the yellow pages under *Leather and Suede Cleaning*.

• **Trust the expert** and respect the advice you're given. These pros know the limitations of leather.

Dyeing Fabrics

An amateur can successfully color a 100% cotton material with a store-bought dye. But for most permanent finishes, dyeing must be attempted at your own risk. If you bought the garment inexpensively secondhand, it's worth a try. However, if you can't afford to ruin the garment, you may want to send it to a professional.

These people may be more successful with the process because they are familiar with the hazards of dyeing synthetics. The technology that produced synthetic fabrics did not as quickly produce the chemicals that could clean, dye and restore synthetics acceptably. Today, some of the technical obstacles to dyeing synthetics have been overcome and they can be dyed professionally. But it's still very difficult, because the fibers are not naturally absorbent. The natural fabrics, wool, silk and cotton, are still the best materials to dye effectively.

Getting clothes dyed by a pro

• **You can mail your garment** to All More Dye House, at 4422 South Wentworth, Chicago, Ill. 60609; (312) 268-5000. They have been in business since 1919 and they'll dye almost any garment. Typical prices at this printing: wool coats, $20.00; jackets, $10.00; and sweaters, $10.00. You pay the mailing expenses, and there's no guarantee given.

• **Or get someone else to mail for you.** If you don't want the hassle of mailing, ask a drycleaner if he or she sends garments to a dyehouse. It will cost more, but the convenience may be more important. Don't be afraid to consider professional dyeing as a money-saving alternative when quality clothing is spotted or faded.

Saving Money on Special Clothes

This chapter will help you get special clothes—for example, for children, pregnant women and the handicapped—for less. If you've ever shopped for clothes in these categories, you know that the retail prices are often quite high. These tips should be real aids in finding new, cheaper sources for these items.

Children's Clothes

The cost of children's clothes has escalated dramatically in the last few years. You can increase the buying power of your clothing dollar by combining second-hand and new clothes for kids (see page 137). You need to know what brands perform best, when you can buy a cheaper product, what to buy second-hand and how to choose sizes that will give you longer wear.

What counts in kids' clothes

• **Look for these major brands** for the best performance: Carters, Healthtex, Sears and Penney's (this applies to both second-hand and new). Good quality is most important for play clothes and everyday infant wear.

• **Choose fabric for wearability and washability.** A good combination of cotton and polyester should save maintenance time (see page 34).

• **Spend less for party or dressy clothes** for tots and infants. You can buy these cheaply at major discount chains. You will also find these clothes in abundance at resale shops. Or let Grandma buy them! (She might be able to find salesmen's sample sales, too.)

• **Buy tube socks** for much more wear per pair.

• **Buy these clothes a size larger** than necessary: coats, jackets (if the shoulders aren't too big), snowpants with adjustable straps, shorts, t-shirts, sweaters, skirts with elastic waistbands, blouses, sundresses with straps and infant sleepers. Your kids will grow into them before you know it!

• **If you don't intend to hem slacks,** don't buy a size larger. If you roll up the cuffs, they come down, the bottom gets frayed and your child stumbles and trips on them.

For added savings

• **Add to the wearability** of your children's clothes by letting down hems, adding fabric to worn hems or pant cuffs, reinforcing the knees on slacks or adding decorative patches. If waists are too loose on slacks and skirts, use a belt or suspenders.

• **Buy uni-sex outfits** in play clothes and outerwear. This works well if you have boys and girls and will be passing the clothes between them.

• **Check catalogs** such as Sears, Penney's or Ward's in August for good sale buys on back-to-school clothes.

• **To save more money,** avoid children's specialty stores while clothes are in season. Do watch for their end-of-season clearances and buy for the next year, however.

Children's shoes

• **Select the correct size** in shoes; they should never be too large.

• **Buy good quality shoes** for play or everyday. But buy second-hand or cheaper brands for dressy shoes that are not worn often.

• **Buy all-cotton or mostly-cotton socks** for better foot comfort.

To Buy or Not to Buy Second-Hand

Most children's clothes can be bought used if they are checked carefully for wear. This list will give you an idea of common items to consider buying second-hand for infants and children. You'll also get some tips on what to avoid.

Buy Second-Hand

Dress-up clothes

Special dress coats

Dress shoes

Infants' undershirts

Receiving blankets

Infants' hats

Jeans for cut-offs

Boots

Don't Buy Second-Hand

Rubber pants

Winter coats and snowsuits. (They're sometimes not as warm as new ones; the stuffing becomes compressed.)

Play pants and shoes are best bought new.

Nightgowns, sleepers and pajamas. (They may have been treated with a flame retardant that has been linked with cancer and was banned in 1977.)

Sport Clothes and Equipment for Children

A good recycling place to buy children's sport equipment and sport clothes is at thrift stores, Goodwill or Salvation Army stores, garage sales and church rummage sales (see page 159). Here is a list of some unusual items you might find.

- Dancing tights, ballet shoes, tap shoes
- Hockey equipment, skates, pucks, sticks, pads
- Baseball shoes, balls, bats, gloves
- Footballs, shoulder pads, knee pads
- Basketballs
- Gym trunks
- Soccer balls
- Skateboards
- Rollerskates
- Figure skates
- Ski equipment, boots, skis, poles
- Bicycles*

*If you are looking for a bicycle, also check out your local police station and ask if they hold bike auctions. Call a skate exchange in your area to trade in skates that are too small, for larger ones. Look in the yellow pages under *Skating Equipment and Supplies*.

Maternity Clothes

This is the time in your life when you really want to look good—but the dilemma is always whether you should spend the money when it's only for nine months! Here are some tips for the mother-to-be that will save you money on maternity dressing and help you look great while doing it.

Dressing for two

It's not necessary to start your shopping in maternity stores. Look through your husband's closet first. Then hit the thrift stores for accessories (see page 106). Go to fabric stores and look at the ribbons and trims. If you don't sew, find someone who does and ask for help.

- **Direct attention to your face** by wearing attractive and colorful scarves and blouses. Keep in mind that you want to balance out your profile (also known as a big tummy).

- **Choose jumpers** as the mainstay for your maternity wardrobe. You can dress them up or down for work and play. Sew them yourself or find a seamstress; try to make three different styles. Pick fabrics that make you feel classy. Lightweight fabrics can double as sundresses in hot weather.

- **Invest in an attractive blouse** with detail at the neck, in a color that flatters you most. You don't need to buy a maternity blouse if you wear jumpers. Unbutton the blouse over your tummy.

• **Buy the stretch tummy inserts** at fabric stores and put them in the jeans or slacks that fit you best. Maternity slacks are too baggy in the seat area for some women.

• **Find elastic-waisted skirts or slacks** for the early months. Wear them again later when the baby is born, until you get back into shape.

• **Give your feet a break.** Buy comfortable, low pumps and sandals. Coordinate them to your non-pregnant wardrobe and remember that you can enjoy them later.

• **Be sporty.** Men's sweatpants and jogging shorts will help you keep active and comfortable. You'll find these in abundance at thrift stores (see page 106).

• **Try your husband's bib overalls** with one of his shirts. Some women I know wore their husbands' jeans, sweaters and shirts all through their pregnancies.

• **Be flexible about coats.** Wearing a coat can be a problem in the later months. Look for pullover sweater shawls and capes that you can also wear post-partum.

Interviewing and Work Clothes

Let your dressing strategy give you an effective edge on interviews and at work. Good wardrobe planning will save you money (see pages 10–14) and dressing time each morning.

Create an effective image

Quality and *conservative* are two important words to remember when you are dressing for job interviews or work.

• **If you can, take a look before the interview** to see how other employees on your job level are dressed. You should be dressed as if you are ready to begin work when you arrive for your interview.

• **Buy quality,** whether it's a new suit or second-hand (see page 27). Go for the rich-looking fabrics and good construction details (see page 29).

• **Dress conservatively.** Traditional-style blazers and suits work best to give you an air of authority. If you are unsure of the classic look in clothing (see pages 42–47), browse through a Brooks Brothers store in your area, or look through the most conservative shop in town.

• **Wear conservative colors:** black, gray, navy, brown or beige. Avoid loud colors and flashy ties that will overwhelm your appearance.

• **Play down accessories.** You don't want to be twisting a necklace or scarf during an interview.

• **Be discreet.** Revealing clothes are *never* appropriate for offices. Don't go braless.

The Big Beautiful Woman

A friend of mine is a size 22½. She says she waited almost half her life to buy clothes, thinking she would do it when she lost weight. Finally she decided to put her size to work for her. She subscribed to the fashion magazine, *Big Beautiful Woman*. However, all she found at first was polyester pantsuits and loose-fitting styles.

If you are over size 16, you know the problem of buying stylish clothes, especially if you want to save money. The principles in building a wardrobe are the same for larger-sized women as they are for smaller-sized women (see pages 7–16). Your best investment is less quantity and more quality. Today, more designers are making clothes for women size 16 and larger. Some names to look for: Joseph Picone, Gloria Vanderbilt, Givenchy, Koret of California, Sharon Rothfeld, Rejoice and Mantessa.

Buy big for less time and money

Your initial investment in better clothing will cost you more money. It's very difficult to find fashionable larger-sized clothing at garage sales or resale shops. These clothes have not been around long enough to be re-cycled second-hand yet, but here are a few tips that will help you in your search.

• **Develop a relationship with a saleslady** at a special-size store. Ask her to call you when a new shipment of clothing in your size arrives and before sales open.

• **Find a good seamstress** —one who can design blouses for you (see page 129). It will be cheaper than buying in the store.

• **Keep alteration possibilities in mind** when you are shopping. If your arms are too large for your suit, have your seamstress alter the sleeves.

• **Buy separates** that will mix and match with at least three other pieces in your wardrobe. It's best to choose three basic colors (for example, gray, blue and cranberry) that look best on you.

• **Shop for shoes at discount shoe stores.** If your foot is not extra-wide, you may be able to buy for a lot less.

• **Write down the name of the manufacturer** or label of any outfit that fits and performs well in your wardrobe. You'll want to search for these items again.

Formal Clothes

Wedding dresses and tuxedos can be an expensive buy when you consider the value per wear (see page 10). I bought my wedding ensemble second-hand. I shopped the bridal stores first and then I checked the want-ads. The same dress and veil I bought for $75.00 second-hand was shown to me at a bridal store for $300.00. After the wedding, one of my bridesmaids bought my dress for $65.00. I saved the floor-length mantilla veil. My value per wear was $10.00.

Before you invest in a tuxedo, wedding gown or evening gown, be sure to consider renting or buying second-hand.

Buy deluxe for fewer bucks

• **Check the newspaper want ads** under *Clothing* for tuxedos, wedding gowns and evening dresses.

• **Phone** thrift stores, dry-cleaners, Salvation Army and Goodwill stores (see page 159) to see if they have the item you need.

• **Look in the phone book's yellow pages** under *Formal* for a store that specializes in formal wear. Check the cost of renting a tux-edo. If you only wear a tux once in a great while, it may be worth it to you to rent. Also ask if the shop sells second-hand tuxedos or wedding gowns.

Furs

The fantasy of owning a fur coat can become a reality even on a low budget. One of my prized "best bargains" is a 1940's mouton coat. I paid $1.75 for the coat at a garage sale. It was in perfect condition and feels great in below-zero weather. On a resale basis I've been offered $50.00 for the coat by several second-hand dealers.

A well-maintained fur does have a resale value. Most fur-riers take old furs in trade and resell them to second-hand dealers. If one of your dreams is to wear a fur coat, check these tips first.

Buying a second-hand fur

• **Browse through the elegant fur stores** in your area. Know the "downtown price" of a new fur, especially the ones you like.

• **Look in the phone book's yellow pages** under *Fur.* A second-hand dealer's ad will usually stress that he or she sells second-hand furs. You can phone the Better Business Bureau to see if they have any complaints registered.

• **Pick a second-hand store that mainly sells furs.** Often you'll find a no re-fund policy, but if you have trouble, a larger second-hand dealer is likelier to try to keep you a happy fur customer.

• **Scout garage sales.** You may find a good deal on a fur at a garage sale or at a Salvation Army store, but make sure you buy it very cheaply. Unless you are a fur expert, you may not be able to spot a rotted fur.

How to examine a fur

• **Check for stress points** on a second-hand fur. Common areas are on the sleeve cuffs, pockets and around the buttons or hooks. Shoulder bags break the fur down at the shoulder point, so check them too.

• **Examine the lining.** Choose a coat with a lining in good condition. It costs well over $100.00 to have a fur coat relined.

• **Pull out the pocket of a fur coat.** If there are a few granules of sawdust inside, this means the coat has been cleaned—sometime! (Fur coats are cleaned by a method that involves sawdust.)

• **Gently stroke the fur** to check its texture. If the fur has guard hairs, you will see a longer layer of fur covering a dense underfur that is lighter in color. This type of fur gives protection from the weather. Flat furs such as lamb, squirrel and rabbit do not have guard hairs; mink is a good example of a fur with guard hair.

• **Know your lifestyle** when you are buying a fur. More durable choices are mink, nutria, raccoon, unsheared beaver and Alaskan seal.

• **Ask the dealer to let out a seam** in the lining. Then examine the skin. A natural fur will have an undyed lining. Some experts say that dyed fur breaks down faster. Also check the skin for softness. There should be no cracking or hardness to the skin.

• **For more information** on buying and maintaining furs, write to the American Fur Industry, 855 Avenue of the Americas, New York City, N.Y., 10001. Ask for the booklet, "Fur Naturally," and include 50¢ for handling costs.

Antique and Vintage Clothing

Vintage clothing connoisseurs search out old fashions by digging through stacks of old clothes at church rummage sales, Salvation Army stores and thrift stores (see page 159). They are trying to beat the high cost of yesterday's threads. Clothing from the 20's to the 50's is in great demand, and the prices reflect this.

You can avoid the digging by shopping antique stores (though not all carry clothing) and vintage specialty shops. Vintage stores clean the clothes, sometimes repair them and give you a little history behind the outfits. But you'll pay for the expertise and convenience, especially in major cities, where there is the greatest interest.

The best of yesterday's threads

You may find flapper dresses from the 20's, beaded evening purses, men's baggy gabardine slacks, women's tailored suits from the 40's and much more. If you are new to the hunt for fashions of the past, these tips will help to get you started.

• **Look in the yellow pages** under *Antiques*, *Clothing* and *Second-Hand Stores* to find the vintage specialty stores in your area.

• **Familiarize yourself with the styles** of these past fashions (see pages 143-147). Shop the specialty stores for ideas. This will give you the shopping edge when you are digging at a rummage sale.

• **Check out all sources:** church rummage sales, Salvation Army and Goodwill stores, thrift stores and garage sales. Sometimes vintage clothes are sold or donated because people don't know their value, so these can be the cheapest sources.

• **Go early to the sales** for the best buys. You will be waiting in line with other collectors, dealers and enthusiasts.

• **Try on all the clothes.** You cannot judge from the marked sizes. This applies to both men's and women's clothing. Some of the larger dresses and slacks look great belted.

• **Always check carefully for wear,** stress and stains (see page 98). Expect to find a certain amount, since after all, some of these clothes are *really* old.

• **Ask the vintage store owners for the names of the cleaners** they use to dryclean their clothes. Some fabric of the 30's and 40's is washable, but if the material is too delicate, you will have to use a drycleaner experienced in cleaning vintage clothes.

A decade of fashion at a glance

If you are interested in getting to know the styles from decades past, look through old *Vogue* magazines at your library. For men's fashions, *The Apparel Arts* magazine dates back to the 30's. You may have to look for these magazines at a university library that specializes in textile design.

1920–1930

1930–1940

1940–1950

1950–1960

1920–1930

- Silhouette was short, straight and simple
- No zippers were used
- Tight-fitting cloche hats
- Long, flowing scarves and feather boas
- Chemise waists on dresses (low on the hips) with pleats dropping from the hips
- Schiaparelli's Trompe L'Oeil hand-knit long tunic sweaters, with scarves tied gypsy-style at the waist
- The flapper dress reigned

1930–1940

- Jean Harlow made the look of the long, white satin, bias-cut gown
- The popular fur was ermine
- Zippers were used for the first time in clothing
- Chanel created the cotton evening dress
- The new ready-to-wear market introduced artificial silks and washable clothes
- Satin shoes and spectator pumps; Ferragamo designed a wedge-heeled evening shoe

1940–1950

• The silhouette was figure-dramatic, with suits pinched tight at the waist and heavily padded shoulders

• Gabardine and flannel were the two most used fabrics

• Anklets were worn with flat sandals and oxford style shoes; nylons were scarce because of the war effort

• Fur paws and tails were draped around suit jackets

• Designer Dior dropped the hemline in the late 40's

1950–1960

• Suit shoulder pads were diminished; the straight skirt took on a curved slimness

• Designer Dior created the "sheath" evening dress

• Later, evening dresses were shown with a stiff balloon design in stiff satins

• Hats were worn with veils covering the whole face

• Designer Dior shortened the skirt length with a waist tucked in above a full skirt over crinolines

• Sweater sets with skirts

1920–1930

- Preppy look, V-neck sweaters with bow ties, tweed knickers
- Tuxedos with elegant tails, top hats, white gloves and white satin scarves
- Spats worn over narrow black simple-lined shoes
- Gatsby-style tailored suits
- Trousers widened into "Oxford bags"
- Huge, bear-like, long-haired raccoon coats
- Slouch hats of "handkerchief felt"

1930–1940

- Double-breasted tweed overcoats
- Double-breasted suits, narrow at the waist
- White gabardine suits
- Flannel straight-legged, cuffed slacks
- Three-piece suits with peaked lapels
- Small-collared, white starched shirts
- Pastel-colored silk stockings with garters
- Oxford shoes with fringed leather tops

1940–1950

- The long four-button "University Jacket" with a center vent in back and small lapels
- Two-button suits with peaked lapels
- "Baggy" gabardine slacks with cuffs
- Pinstripe suits
- Wide-spread collars on white shirts
- Crew-neck sweaters, V-neck sweater vests
- Loafers, leisure shoes with a slight wedge

1950–1960

- The suit took on a "natural" look: two-button and three-button single-breasted suits with a straight, hanging jacket
- Suit material was lightweight
- Slip-on shoes came into being; loafers of all styles were popular
- Washable long-sleeved sports shirts with bigger collars in a "silkanese" fabric
- Rayon shirts with small designs worn with sportcoats

Clothing for the Handicapped

There are no patterns available from the major companies to help you make clothing for the handicapped. If you are handicapped, you already know the problems you are faced with in clothing. But if you are sewing for a handicapped individual or have a handicapped child, these tips should give you a lot of new pointers. The information here is for the wheelchair-bound individual who is not severely disabled. (See page 154 for sewing and buying aids for handicapped clothing.)

Mariam Strebel, an occupational therapist, nurse and clothing consultant for the Sister Kenney Institute in Minneapolis, Minnesota, has given her expertise to this section.

Special clothing tips

• **Dress simply,** since it is easier to look neat when seated if the lines are uncluttered. Choose tops that don't easily bunch up. Stay away from long jackets and bulky sweaters or cardigans. Wear vests, form-fitting sweaters and blouses, or suit jackets that are cut short.

• **Stick with colors in the same color family** for a more unified look.

• **Look for slacks that will give you good thigh spread** (this is important for circulation), but don't wear the rest of the slack too wide at the bottom —it looks sloppy. If you find the correct fit in the thigh, you can have the bottom of the slacks altered. Do make sure the slacks are long enough to cover your ankles.

• **Avoid back zippers.** Women can dress up with a long dress or skirt with side zipper. (These are abundant in second-hand stores.)

• **Choose open-backed shoes** to avoid swollen ankles.

• **Hang a back pack on the back of your wheelchair** to carry personal items.

• **Choose fabrics in 100% natural material** that will breathe, rather than synthetics that may be too hot.

• **Avoid bulky coats or jackets.** Try wearing a down vest, poncho or shawl.

Bargain Accessories

For years, fashion models have been shopping thrift stores and dime stores for bargain accessories. It may take more time to do so, but you can save a lot of money—and even *make* money (by watching for items to resell). Whenever you pick up a fashion magazine, look at the accessorizing ideas as you study the fashions and outfits. That knowledge, plus the tips in this chapter, should make you a smart bargain accessory buyer and wearer.

Classic Accessories

Accessory styles often make comebacks in the fashion scene. A couple of years ago, pearl chokers were the big accessory statement for women. I bought mine at a rummage sale for 75¢. Take advantage of fashion repeaters and buy them cheaply second-hand (see page 48). At such bargain prices, there's no reason why you can't have accessories for every outfit!

Dual Purpose Accessories

You can give an accessory a new job and increase its function in your wardrobe.

• **Use a pair of clip-on earrings** as cuff links, or clip them onto a pair of shoes for a dressy look.

• **Wrap a pearl choker around your wrist** as a bracelet.

• **Pin a pretty pierced earring** to a blazer, scarf or hat.

• **Add a silk flower** to a haircomb, belt or purse. Or wrap it around your wrist as a bracelet.

• **Use a man's tie** as a belt.

Common Bargain Accessories

• **Jewelry:** pearls, rhinestones, unique costume jewelry.

• **Purses:** small clutch evening bags and unique handmade purses.

• **Belts:** all colors and shapes: evening belts, sport belts, men's belts. Most belts are labeled on the inside if they are leather.

• **Scarves:** all types, in silk, nylon and wool. All styles, from Western bandannas to long Gatsby scarves. Often the scarves have never been worn.

• **Men's ties:** many sizes, colors and fabrics. Don't buy a tie that's stained. Look for the 100% silk ties (there is usually a small fabric label at the inside tip of the tie). Check the inside of a vintage tie lining—you may find a picture of a nude woman! These ties are collectors' items and are quite rare, but I always look!

Quick Scarf Tricks

Using a little imagination with scarves, you can multiply and brighten your wardrobe very inexpensively. All it takes is a little know-how and a scarf. You can easily wrap and tie a large oblong or square scarf around your waist. Here are some other tricks to try.

• **Design a halter bra:** take two 36-inch square scarves. Fold one of them to wrap around your bosom, and tie it in the back. Take the second scarf, fold and twist it, then pull this second scarf through the center of the first scarf. Tie it around your neck.

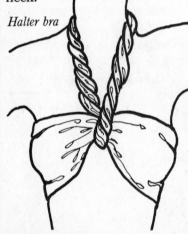

Halter bra

• **Wrap your head:** using a square scarf, fold opposite corners together to form a triangle (this is unnecessary if you're using an oblong). Place the center of the triangle on the top of your head; then push it down low over your forehead. Take the ends of the triangle and tie them behind your head. Twist these ends into ropes and tie them at the center of your forehead. Tuck all the leftover end-pieces under the scarf.

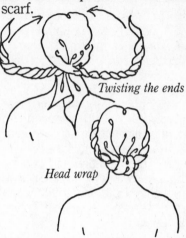

Twisting the ends

Head wrap

• **Make a necklace:** use a 22" square scarf. Fold the two triangle tips together; then fold the scarf in half. Tie a big knot in the center of the folded scarf. Place the scarf around your neck, with the knot in front. Twist the tails, and tie at the back of your neck. Tuck the leftover flaps under the scarf.

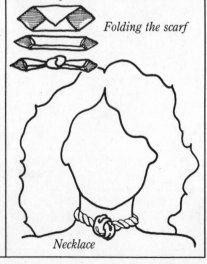

Folding the scarf

Necklace

- **Tie an ascot:** use an oblong scarf. Tie it around your neck and knot it in front. Loop one end of the scarf over the knot, and spread out the top fold of the scarf to cover the knot.

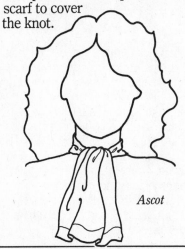

Ascot

Jewelry

You can really put some gold in your jewelry box for just nickels and dimes. My favorite shopping places are garage sales and thrift stores. At one garage sale in California, I bought a pair of 10 karat gold earrings for 75¢.

When you shop for bargain accessories and jewelry, remember to bring a small magnifying glass with you. It will help you read the markings and determine values. The following tips will tell you what to look for.

Gold

For about the last 40 years, jewelers have had to follow strict gold marking regulations. Old gold that was fashioned over 40 years ago is not always honestly marked.

- **Karats.** In jewelry, pure gold is alloyed with other metals for hardness. The karat mark (K) identifies the percentage of gold in an item. An item marked 24K is made of 100% pure gold. Other karat designations are 10K, 14K, 18K and 22K. In the United States, nothing less than 10 karats can be called "gold" or "karat gold." In England, 9K gold is available.

- **Filling and washing.** Gold-filled jewelry usually contains more gold than electroplated gold items do. Sometimes you will find a sterling piece that has been "gold-washed." The content of gold in "gold-wash" is even less than in an electroplated item. The most common colors of gold in jewelry are white and yellow; you may also find red and green gold.

Sterling silver

Sterling is always marked as such on jewelry. Many screw-on earrings of the 40's and 50's (common finds in second-hand sources) have sterling backs. You will find the *sterling* marking in tiny print on the screw part of the earring.

- **Mexican silver** is similar to American sterling, but it's yellowish in appearance. It's not marked *sterling*; rather it's marked *Mexico* and sometimes has the number 925 stamped on it as well.

Pearls

Pearls are found in many colors, from white to pastels to black. Little scuffs and irregularities are part of a natural pearl's surface. Cultured pearls (which are also "real" pearls) are matched pretty closely in size and shape.

- **Pearl necklaces** that have a knot between each pearl are considered a better quality item. You'll see this in both real and fake pearl jewelry, but chances are good that if there is a knot in between, it may be a real pearl.

- **Clasps.** Another clue to look for is when the clasp is set with a gem and the metal is 14K gold or sterling.

- **To check whether pearls are real,** rub them across your teeth. If it feels gravelly instead of smooth, it's probably the real thing. Fake pearls are coated. You can look for signs of chipping on the coating, often around the hold of the pearl.

Rhinestones

There are rhinestones and there are rhinestones.

- **A better rhinestone** will be secured into a necklace, bracelet, pin or earring with small prongs (the more the better), rather than glue.

- **If you see a pin with the name Eisenberg on the back,** buy it. Twenty-five years ago, an Eisenberg pin cost about $25.00. Today at an antique

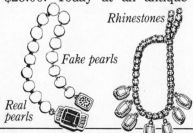

Rhinestones

Fake pearls

Real pearls

store, you will pay from $85.00 to $125.00 for the same pin. It has a beautiful sparkle to the cut, is usually backed with a white metal and looks fantastic on a basic black suit.

Jet

This stone, made out of coal, has been used since ancient times. It has been called "mourning jewelry." The stone was very popular during the 30's, especially in art-deco jewelry; it was also worn during World War II. You will find it in earrings, necklaces, bracelets and pins. Jet is pure black and retains its sparkling polish for many years. Imitation jet will crack, scratch and become dull.

- **If you find what looks like a jet piece,** try touching it to your face: if it feels cold and remains cold it's probably jet.

Platinum

This was considered the prestigious metal for jewelry in the 30's. Many high-society figures of the time (such as the Whitneys and Vanderbilts) wore platinum jewelry, often in a filigree style on rings, necklaces, bracelets and earrings. Platinum is an expensive, hard and elegant metal with a gray, dull cast to it.

- **In a quality diamond ring,** the prongs holding the diamond are often made of platinum.

- **Platinum jewelry** is identified by the marking: 10% IRID—PLAT. Occasionally it will be marked only PLAT.

Appendix

Useful Resources

Fashion

Books

Fashion Smarts, by Kristen Brown and Susan Cooney-Evans (Playboy Paperbacks, 1980).

Manstyle, by Peter Carlsen and William Wilson (Clarkson N. Potter, 1977).

Dress for Success, by John T. Molloy (Warner Books, 1978).

The Woman's Dress for Success Book, by John T. Molloy (Warner Books, 1978).

Glamour's Success Book, by Barbara Coffey (Simon & Schuster, 1979).

Womanstyle, by Leah Feldon (Clarkson N. Potter, 1979).

The Power Look, by Egon Von Furstenberg with Camille Duhe (Holt, Rinehart & Winston, 1978).

Cheap Chic, by Catherine Milinaire and Carol Troy (Harmony Book, 1976).

In Vogue, by Georgina Howell (Penguin, 1978).

Fashion of the Thirties, by Julian Robinson (Two Continents Publishing Group, 1978).

Fashion in the Forties, by Julian Robinson (St. Martin's Press, 1976).

Sewing for the Outdoors, by Hal Bennett (Clarkson N. Potter, 1980).

Working Wardrobe, by Janet Wallach (Acropolis Books, 1981).

Magazines for Women

Glamour
Harper's Bazaar
Ladies Home Journal
McCall's
Mademoiselle
Essence
Seventeen
Vogue
Big Beautiful Woman
Cosmopolitan
Working Woman
Town & Country

Magazines for Men

Gentleman's Quarterly
Playboy
Essence
Esquire
Apparel Arts

Clothing maintenance

The Stain Removal Handbook, by Max and Simon Alth (Hawthorn Books, 1978).

Spot Check: How to Cope with Household Stains, by Nina Grunfeld and Michael Thomas (Price/Stern/Sloan, 1981).

Finance information

Guide to Wise Buying, by The Better Business Bureau (The Benjamin Company, 1980).

New Money Book for the 80's, by Sylvia Porter (Doubleday, 1979).

Marketplace information

The Wholesale by Mail Catalog, by Lowell Miller (St. Martin's Press, 1979).

Good Garb, by William Nathan Dasheff and Laura Dearborn (Dell, 1980).

The Barter Way to Beat Inflation, by George W. Burtt (Everest House, 1980).

The Good Buy Book, by Annie Moldafsky—6-State Edition (Illinois, Indiana, Michigan, Minnesota, Ohio, Wisconsin); (Rand McNally, 1980).

Shopping source guides

Save On Shopping Directory, by Iris Ellis, S.O.S., P.O. Box 10482, Dept. DL, Jacksonville, FL 32207 ($6.95).

Budget Shoppers Guide to the Delaware Valley, by Thomas L. Widing (Delaware); (Hamilton House, 1976).

Bargain Hunting in L.A., by Barbara Patridge (California); (J.P. Tarcher, 1976).

The Manhattan Clothes Shopping Guide, by Elaine Louie (Macmillan, 1978).

FOSG Publications, Box 239, Oradell, NJ 07649 (Factory outlet shopping guides for the following areas: North and South Carolina, Pennsylvania, Washington DC, Maryland, Delaware, Virginia).

Bird Associates Inc., 449 Second Street, Oradell, NJ 07649 (Factory outlet shopping guides for the following areas: New England; New Jersey and Rockland County, New York; New York, Long Island, Westchester; North and South Carolina; Pennsylvania; Washington DC, Maryland, Delaware, Virginia).

Special Sources for the Handicapped

Here's some information that will aid you in sewing and buying clothing for the handicapped.

Mail order sources

Clothing for Handicapped People, c/o Naomi Reich, School of Home Economics, University of Arizona, Tucson, AZ 85721. (This book covers all the mail order sources for handicapped clothing in the country. It was compiled by Naomi Reich, Patricia Otten and Marie Negri Carver.)

Clothing for the Handicapped: Fashion Adaptations for Adults and Children, c/o Sister Kenny Institute, Publications A/V Dept., Abbott Northwestern Hospital, Chicago Ave. at 27th St., Minneapolis, MN 55407. (Cost: $3.00, plus $1.00 for handling. This is a book for the home sewer who wants to adapt patterns.)

Donna Karal Company, 331 S.W. Fifth Ave., Cambridge, MN 55008, (612) 689–3468 or (612) 689–3974. (Clothing is designed especially for handicapped adults, children and nursing-home patients. These items are moderately expensive, but the work is excellent. You can custom-order to fit your needs.)

I Can Do It Myself, 3773 Peppertree Dr., Eugene, OR 97402, (503) 342–2997 or (503) 687–0119. (This company carries a nice selection of children's and adults' clothes, reasonably priced.)

Mail Order Directory

It's fun to receive catalogs, and you can save a lot of time if you do your shopping through them. Use your catalogs as a guide to fashion. Compare the prices to your local store prices before you order.

* = an exceptional bargain

ACORN PRODUCTS COMPANY
390 Central Ave.
Lewiston, ME 04240
(207) 784-9412/9186
(hand-knit hats and scarves)

*ANDEAN PRODUCTS
Apartado 472
Cuenca, Ecuador
(heavy sweaters of thick wool)

*JOS. A. BANK CLOTHIERS, INC.
109 Market Pl.
Baltimore, MD 21202
(301) 837-1700
(men's clothing)

EDDIE BAUER
Fifth and Union
P.O. Box 3700
Seattle, WA 98124
(800) 426-8020
(outdoor and down clothing)

L.L. BEAN
Freeport, ME 04033
(207) 865-3111
(outdoor outfitters)

BERGMAN COMPANY
P.O. Box 56
East Lempster, NH 03605
(603) 863-3646
(sweaters)

BRIGADE QUARTERMASTER
P.O. Box 108
Powder Springs, GA 30073
(404) 943-9336
(surplus and military clothing)

BRITISH ISLES COLLECTION
115 Brand Rd.
Salem, VA 24156
(703) 389-2814
(men's and women's clothing)

*I. BUSS
738 Broadway
New York, NY 10003
(212) 242-3338
(uniform and surplus clothing)

CABLE CAR CLOTHIERS
150 Post St.
San Francisco, CA 94108
(415) 397-7733
(men's and women's clothing)

CASCO BAY TRADING POST
Freeport, ME 04032
(207) 865-6371
(outdoor clothing)

*V. JUUL CHRISTENSEN AND SON
17 Livjacgergade
DK-2100 Copenhagen
Denmark
Discount: 30 to 50%
(Icelandic sweaters, ponchos, pullovers, scarves and hats)

DENNIS CONNOR
1444 Pioneer Way
El Cajon, CA 92020
(714) 440-2324
(sailing and casual clothes)

COUNTRY STORE OF CONCORD
15 Monument St.
Concord, MA 01742
(614) 486-9211
(women's clothing, some men's clothing)

*COUNTRY WAYS
3500 Hwy. 101 South
Minnetonka, MN 55343
(612) 473-4334
(easy-to-make kits)

DANNER SHOES
P.O. Box 22204
Portland, OR 97222
(503) 653-2920
(footwear)

***DAVID AND JOE
TRADING CO.**
P.O. Box 8189
Shamshuipo, Kowloon
Hong Kong
Discount: 30 to 90%
(beaded and embroidered
sweaters, bags and gloves)

*DEFENDER INDUSTRIES
255 Main St.
P.O. Box 820
New Rochelle, NY 10801
(boating clothes)

DUNHAM'S OF MAINE
Waterville, ME 04901
(207) 873-6165
(men's and women's clothing)

EARLY WINTERS LTD.
110 Prefontaine Pl. S.
Seattle, WA 98104
(206) 622-5203
(outdoor equippers)

**EASTERN MOUNTAIN
SPORTS, INC.**
Vose Farm Rd.
Peterborough, NH 03458
(603) 924-9212
(outdoor equippers)

FELLMAN SHOES
12 East 46th St./24 East 44th St.
New York, NY 10017
(212) 682-3144
(importers of Lotus
Veldtschoens)

C.C. FILSON
205 Maritime Bldg.
Seattle, WA 98104
(206) 624-4437
(outdoor clothing)

*HY FISHMAN FURS
305 Seventh Ave.
New York, NY 10001
(212) 244-4948
(furs)

**FRENCH CREEK SHEEP
AND WOOL CO.**
Elverson, PA 19520
(215) 286-5700
(shearling coats, natural oiled
wool sweaters)

FROSTLINE KITS
Frostline Circle
Denver, CO 80241
(303) 451-5600
(kits for outdoor gear and
clothing)

GANDER MOUNTAIN
P.O. Box 248
Wilmot, WI 53192
(800) 558-9410
(general outdoor outfitters)

GOKEYS
P.O. Box 43659/84
South Wabasha St.
St. Paul, MN 55107
(612) 292-3911
(men's and women's clothing)

*GOLDBERGS' MARINE
202 Market St.
Philadelphia, PA 19106
(sweaters)

**GREAT PACIFIC
IRONWORKS**
P.O. Box 150
Ventura, CA 93001
(800) 235-3371
(outdoor clothes and
climbing gear)

HARBORSIDE SHOP
Bay View St.
Camden, ME 04843
(207) 236-4567
(outdoor clothes)

**HOLUBAR
MOUNTAINEERING LTD.**
P.O. Box 7
Boulder, CO 80306

(800) 525-2540
(outdoor equippers, down
clothing)

*HUDSON'S
105 Third Ave.
New York, NY 10003
(212) 475-9568
Catalog: $1.00
Discount: up to 40% (clothing
for camping and casual wear)

*ICEMART
P.O. Box 23
Keflavik International Airport
Iceland
Catalog: $1 airmail
Discount: minimum 30%
(sweaters)

**INTERNATIONAL
MOUNTAIN EQUIPMENT**
P.O. Box 494, Main St.
North Conway, NH 03860
(603) 356-5287
(outdoor equippers and climbing
gear)

**KALPAKIAN KNITTING
MILLS**
605 West Eighth Ave.
Vancouver, B.C. V5Z 1C7
(604) 873-4717
(virgin wool sweaters and socks)

**H. KAUFFMAN & SONS
SADDLERY CO.**
139 East 24th St.
New York, NY 10010
(212) 684-6060
(men's, women's and children's
western wear)

KOMITO BOOTS
P.O. Box 2106
Estes Park, CO 80517
(303) 586-5391
(mountain footwear)

KREEGER & SON
16 West 46th St.
New York, NY 10036
(212) 575-7825
(outdoor outfitters)

LADY MADONNA
36 East 31st St.

New York, NY 10016
(212) 685-4555
(maternity clothes)

*LAURENCE CORNER
62/64 Hampstead Rd.
London NW1 2NU
England
Catalog: $2.50
(surplus goods and clothing)

PETER LIMMER & SONS
Intervale, NH 03845
(603) 356-5378
(hiking boots)

LOWE ALPINE SYSTEMS
P.O. Box 189
Lafayette, CO 80026
(800) 525-2945
(mountaineering clothes and
equipment)

**D. MACGILLIVRAY
AND COY**
Muir of Aird
Benbecual
Western Isles, Scotland
PA88 5NA
(clothing for men, women and
children)

**MARMOT MOUNTAIN
WORKS**
331 South 13th St.
Grand Junction, CO 81501
(800) 525-7070
(down and outdoor clothing)

**McCREEDY &
SCHREIBER**
37 West 46th St./55 West
46th St.
New York, NY 10036
(212) 582-1552
(Lucchese boots)

RANDAL MERRELL
228 South 1500 West
Vernal, UT 84078
(801) 789-3079
(custom-made handcrafted
hiking and western boots)

MOOR AND MOUNTAIN
63 Park St.
Andover, MA 01810

(617) 475-3665
(outdoor outfitters)

MOTHERCARE-BY-MAIL
P.O. Box 3881
New York, NY 10017
(212) 490-9095
(clothing for mother and baby)

ORVIS
Manchester, VT 05254
(802) 362-1300
(outdoor equippers)

CARROLL REED
CRSS, Dept. 77001
North Conway, NH 03860
(classic sportswear for men,
women and children)

**REI (RECREATIONAL
EQUIPMENT, INC.)**
P.O. Box C-88125
Seattle, WA 98188
(800) 426-4840
(outdoor equippers)

**ROBBINS
MOUNTAINGEAR/
MOUNTAINWEAR**
Box 4536
Modesto, CA 95352
(209) 529-6913
(sweaters and mountaineering
clothes)

RUGGED WEAR LTD.
Narragansett, RI 02882
(401) 789-4115
(rugby shirts, shorts and
trousers)

W.C. RUSSELL
285 S.W. Franklin
Berlin, WI 54923
(414) 361-2252
(handcrafted moccasins, boots
and shoes)

SIERRA DESIGNS
247 Fourth St.
Oakland, CA 94607
(800) 227-1120
(outdoor clothing)

THE SKI HUT
P.O. Box 309

1615 University Ave.
Berkeley, CA 94701
(415) 843-8170
(outdoor clothing)

SOUSA & LEFKOVITS
GL2
621 S. B Street
Tustin, CA 92680
(traditional clothing for men and
women)

SPIEGEL INC.
P.O. Box 6340
Chicago, IL 60607
Catalog: $3
(men's, women's and children's
clothes; home furnishings)

STAFFORDS
P.O. Box 2055/808 Smith Ave.
Thomasville, GA 31792
(912) 226-4306
(outdoor clothing)

TALBOTS
164 North St.
Hingham, MA 02043
(617) 749-7830
(women's clothing and some
men's clothing)

NORM THOMPSON
P.O. Box 3999
Portland, OR 97208
(800) 547-1160/1532
(men's and women's clothing)

TODD'S
5 South Wabash Ave.
Chicago, IL 60603
(312) 372-1335
(Chippewa footwear)

U.S. CAVALRY STORE
1375 North Wisom Rd.
Radcliff, KY 40160
(502) 351-1164
(military clothing and accessories)

**WHOLE EARTH
PROVISIONS CO.**
2410 San Antonio St.
Austin, TX 78705
(512) 478-1577
(outdoor clothing)

Source Directory for New and Second-Hand Clothes

The following directory is a selective, incomplete list of a wide variety of sources for new and second-hand clothes in the United States and Canada. It is organized alphabetically by state and city names. Letters in the left margin identify the type of store (DD = Designer Discount; G = Goodwill; J = Junior League; O = Outlet; R = Resale; SA = Salvation Army). If you have any suggestions for sources to add to this list, please send the name of the store and any other pertinent information to Meadowbrook Press, Dept. DBFL, 18318 Minnetonka Blvd., Deephaven, MN 55391. Use this directory to plan your shopping strategy, both at home and on trips, and you'll be sure to dress better for less!

ALABAMA

Athens
O   Athens Lingerie Mill Outlet (underwear for the entire family; discount: 50%)

SA, G   **Birmingham**
O   Brenda Allen's (junior and misses'; discount: 30–65%)
O   Goofs Factory Outlet Pants Place (selected factory irregulars; discount: 50%)
DD   Loehmann's (women's clothing; discount: 20–70%)
J   Nearly New Shop

Huntsville
O   Clara's Name Brand Discount Shoes (men's and women's better-brand shoes; discount: 40–60%)

Lineville
O   Man's World (complete men's wardrobe needs; discount: 30–50%)

G   **Mobile**
O   Goofs Factory Outlet Pants Place (selected factory irregulars; discount: 50%)
J   The Junior League Shop

G   **Montgomery**
O   Brenda Allen's (junior and misses'; discount: 30–65%)
O   Goofs Factory Outlet Pants Place (selected factory irregulars; discount: 50%)
R   Maris' Resale Shoppe, 4309 Atlanta Hwy., (205) 277–4718
R   Re Sale Mart, 408 N. Lawrence, (205) 265–1923

ALASKA

Anchorage
R   Bishop's Attic, 700 E. Firewood La., (907) 279–6328; (clothing for the entire family)
R   The Second Hand, 3920 Mountain View Dr., (907) 276–3924
R   Vickie's "Clothes" Encounter, 8867 Jewel Lake Rd., (907) 243–8935

ARIZONA

G   **Flagstaff**
Glendale
O   Sun City Fashions (junior and women's wear; discount: 25–50%)
Mesa
O   Ashley's—The Outlet Store (family apparel; discount: 50–60%)
O   Sun City Fashions (junior and women's wear; discount: 25–50%)

SA, G   **Phoenix**
R   Encore Boutique, 2913 N. 24th St., (602) 955–7380
O   Grunwald-Marx (men's knit

DD = Designer Discount; G = Goodwill; J = Junior League; O = Outlet; R = Resale; SA = Salvation Army.

shirts, some accessories; discount: 30–50%)

DD　Loehmann's (women's clothing; discount: 20–70%)

DD　Marshall's (men's, women's and children's clothes; discount: 20–70%)

R　The Nearly New Store, 2615 W. Glendale Ave., (602) 242–2000

O　Sun City Fashions (junior and women's wear; discount: 25–50%)

R　Tracy's Nearly-Nu Shop, 5612 E. Thomas Rd., (602) 944–9722

R　Whatnots for Tots, 2401 N. 32nd St., (602) 956–4396

Prescott

O　Sun City Fashions (junior and women's wear; discount: 25–50%)

Scottsdale

O　Novis Deene (women's clothes; discount: 30–70%)

O　Sun City Fashions (junior and women's wear; discount: 25–50%)

Tempe

O　Sun City Fashions (junior and women's wear; discount: 25–50%)

SA, G　**Tucson**

ARKANSAS

Beebe

O　Suburban Casuals Factory Outlet (samples, factory remnants; discount: 30–60%)

Fort Smith

J　Bargain Box

O　Hidden Closet (women's and children's clothing; discount: 50%)

Jonesboro

O　Little Red Shoe House (men's, women's and children's shoes; discount: 20–50%)

SA, G　**Little Rock**

R　Encore Boutique, 2913 N. 24th St., (501) 955–7380

R　Poor Little Rich Girl, Inc., 2804 Kavanaugh Blvd., (501) 664–4440

R　Clothes Closet, 9813 W. Markham, (501) 225–3140

Mammoth Spring

O　Karl's Factory Outlet (women's clothing; discount: 40–75%)

Mena

O　Leather Shoppe (handbags, other accessories; discount: 20–75%)

CALIFORNIA

SA　**Anaheim**

SA　**Bakersfield**

Canoga Park

DD　Marshall's (men's, women's and children's clothes; discount: 20–70%)

SA　**Costa Mesa**

Culver City

O　Jonathan Logan Fabric Warehouse (discount: 10–30%)

Daly City

DD　Loehmann's (women's clothing; discount: 20–70%)

SA　**El Cajon**

El Monte

O　Alex Colman—The Outlook I and II (Mr. Alex brand; discount: 30–50%)

SA　**Fresno**

R　Bunters New & Used Clothing, 2429 E. Belmont Ave., (209) 237–1965

Fullerton

DD　Loehmann's (women's clothing; discount: 20–70%)

Granada Hills

DD　Marshall's (men's, women's and children's clothes; discount: 20–70%)

Huntington Beach

DD　Marshall's (men's, women's and children's clothes; discount: 20–70%)

Laguna Hills

DD　Marshall's (men's, women's and children's clothes; dis-

DD = Designer Discount; G = Goodwill; J = Junior League; O = Outlet; R = Resale; SA = Salvation Army.

count: 20–70%)

La Jolla

R Your Favorite Things, 5645 La Jolla Blvd., (714) 459-0311

La Mirada

DD Marshall's (men's, women's and children's clothes; discount: 20–70%)

SA, G **Long Beach**

O Alex Colman—The Outlook I and II (Mr. Alex brand; discount: 30–50%)

SA, G **Los Angeles**

R Cinema Glamour Shop (Affiliate of Motion Picture and TV Fund), 127 N. LaBrea Ave., (213) 933-5289

O Egelhoff-Kids Hangups (babies to size 20; discount: 10–50%)

J Just the Answer

O Kids Mart (infant to size 14 brand-name clothes; discount: 30–70%)

R Kotik's Clothing, 1233 Vine, (213) 463-3746

R La Jan Recycling with a Touch of Class, 1174 La-Brea Ave., (213) 933-9883

DD Loehmann's (women's clothing; discount: 20–70%)

O Margaret's Kiddie Korner (brand names; discount: 30–40%)

R Patina, 511 S. Glendale Ave., (213) 246-7018

R Peabody's, 1102½ S. La-Cienega Blvd., (213) 652-3810 (vintage clothing for men)

O Shoe Bazaar (sample sizes in European shoes; discount: 40–70%)

R Stars & Debs, 12424 Ventura Blvd., Studio City, (213) 980-7433

R Twotimer, 142 N. Maryland Ave., (213) 242-1650

SA **Lytton (Healdsburg)**

North Hollywood

O Jantzen, Inc. (women's tennis, golf wear, swimsuits,

slacks; discount: 40–75%)

SA, G **Oakland**

J The Shop

SA **Oceanside**

Palo Alto

J The Discovery Shop

SA **Pasadena**

J The Clothes Line

Reseda

DD Loehmann's (women's clothing; discount: 20–70%)

Riverside

DD The Bargain Center

SA, G **Sacramento**

R Act II For Her, 1729 Howe Ave., (916) 920-5821

R Act II For Him, 1735 Howe Ave., (916) 929-2282

DD Marshall's (men's, women's and children's clothes; discount: 20–70%)

R Once Over, 2598 21st St., (916) 456-1719

R Small World Used Children's Clothing, 3442 Mission Ave., (916) 483-8822

SA, G **San Bernardino**

O The Company Store (men's and boys' clothing; discount: 50%)

SA, G **San Diego**

R Chic to Chic, 4880 Cass St., (714) 272-3005

O Kids Mart (infant to size 14 brand-name clothes; discount: 30–70%)

R Marie's Resale Shop, 1225 Garnet Ave., (714) 272-6575

DD Marshall's (men's, women's and children's clothes; discount: 20–70%)

O Men's Fashion Depot (brand name suits, sportscoats, slacks; discount: 40–60%)

O Shoe Paradise (women's and children's shoes; discount: 30–60%)

SA, G **San Francisco**

R Abbe's Nearly New Apparel, 1420 Clement, (415) 751-4567

DD = Designer Discount; G = Goodwill; J = Junior League; O = Outlet; R = Resale; SA = Salvation Army.

R	The Encore, 302 23rd Ave., (415) 221–5242
O	Joseph Magnin (women's clothes and accessories, some designer names; discount: 35–65%)
R	Kidstuff, 1307 Castro, (415) 824–0889
J	Next to New Shop

San Jose SA, G

DD	Marshall's (men's, women's and children's clothes; discount: 20–70%)

SA, G **Santa Ana**

SA **Santa Barbara**

G **Santa Cruz**

SA **Santa Monica**

G **Santa Rosa**

SA, G **Stockton**

Sunnyvale

DD	Loehmann's (women's clothing; discount: 20–70%)

SA **Van Nuys**

COLORADO

Boulder

O	Factory Ski Wear Outlet (all types of ski wear; discount: 50%)

SA, G **Colorado Springs**

O	Jo Ann's Fashion (name brands; discount: 50%)

SA, G **Denver**

R	Elite Repeat Shack, 1468 Iola, (303) 364–6065 (women's and children's clothing)
O	Fabric Outlet Discount Store (fabric and accessories)
J	Junior League Thrift Shop
DD	Loehmann's (women's clothing; discount: 20–70%)
O	Neil's Famous Footwear (cancellations from large stores; discount: 30–60%)
O	Outlet Store (surplus clothing;
O	Sample Simon (sample clothing; discount: 30–70%)
R	Second Look, Ltd., 2328 E. Exposition (303) 777–2473

G **Pueblo**

CONNECTICUT

Avon

DD	Marshall's (men's, women's and children's clothes; discount: 20–70%)

SA, G **Bridgeport**

O	Carolina Factory Outlet (men's and women's shoes; discount: 33–70%)
O	Levine Coat Company (women's and children's clothing; discount: 40%)
O	Warnaco Outlet Store (men's, women's and boys' apparel; discount: 50%)

SA **Bristol**

R	The Cinderella Shoppe, 99 Maple, (203) 589–4813

SA **Brockton**

Cheshire

DD	Marshall's (men's, women's and children's clothes; discount: 20–70%)

SA **Danbury**

O	Grand Fashion (women's clothes; discount: 30–50%)
DD	Marshall's (men's, women's and children's clothes; discount: 20–70%)

Farmington

DD	Loehmann's (women's clothing; discount: 20–70%)

Hamden

DD	Marshall's (men's, women's and children's clothes; discount: 20–70%)

SA **Hartford**

R	Act II Resale Dress & Boutique Shoppe, 149 Park Rd., West Hartford, (203) 233–7125
J	The Clothes Horse
R	Upper Window Resale Dress Shop, 957 Farmington Ave., West Hartford, (203) 232–9617

SA **Manchester**

DD	Marshall's (men's, women's and children's clothes; discount: 20–70%)

SA **Middletown**

DD = Designer Discount; G = Goodwill; J = Junior League; O = Outlet; R = Resale; SA = Salvation Army.

SA **New Britain**
SA, G **New Haven**
O   Only Shirts (specializing in shirts for the big or tall man; discount: 30–60%)

SA, G **New London**
SA **Norwalk**
DD Loehmann's (women's clothing; discount: 20–70%)
    Norwich
O   Gordon Shoe Outlet (seconds, name brands; discount: 20–50%)
    Orange
DD Loehmann's (women's clothing; discount: 20–70%)
DD Marshall's (men's, women's and children's clothes; discount: 20–70%)
    Rockville
O   Roosevelt Mills Factory Outlet (sweaters; discount: 50%)
    Stamford
J   Yellow Balloon
    Stratford
O   Shoetown (name-brand shoes; discount: up to 50%)
SA **Waterbury**
    Watertown
DD Marshall's (men's, women's and children's clothes; discount: 20–70%)
    Wethersfield
DD Marshall's (men's, women's and children's clothes; discount: 20–70%)
SA **Willimantic**
    Windsor
DD Loehmann's (women's clothing; discount: 20–70%)

DELAWARE
SA **Harrington**
    Lewes
O   Dressco, Inc. (ladies' dresses and sports outfits; discount: 40%)
SA **Smyrna**
SA, G **Wilmington**
O   Fairfax Shopping Center

(men's and women's shoes; discount: 30%)
O   Shoe Box, Inc. (women's and children's shoes; discount: 30–60%)

SA, G **DISTRICT OF COLUMBIA**
O   Gerry's Discount (shoes for men, women and children; discount: 30–60%)
O   Heel 'N Toe, Inc. (American and imported women's shoes; discount: 60%)
J   Junior League Shop

FLORIDA
Clearwater
J   Junior League Thrift Shop
O   The Shoe Plaza (women's shoes direct from the manufacturer; discount: 30–70%)
    Deerfield Beach
O   Fashion Warehouse (men's and ladies' clothes; discount: 30–70%)
SA, G **Fort Lauderdale**
J   Junior League Thrift Shop
O   Men's Room and Ladies' Room (men's and women's clothing; discount: 35–60%)
    Fort Myers
O   Found Money Ladies' Shoppe (name-brand women's clothing; discount: 25–75%)
    Gainesville
J   Junior League Thrift Shop
    Hallandale
O   Michael's (brand-name ladies' wear; discount: 20–50%)
DD Syms Clothing, Inc. (men's, women's and children's clothes; discount: 30–60%)
    Hollywood
O   Uncle Fred's Childrens Wear (boys' and girls' clothing, sizes 1–16; discount: 25–35%)
SA, G **Jacksonville**
J   Junior League Thrift Shop
O   Men's Wear Outlet (men's clothes; discount: 30–70%)
R   New to You, 7210 Atlantic

DD = Designer Discount; G = Goodwill; J = Junior League; O = Outlet; R = Resale; SA = Salvation Army.

Blvd., (904) 724–3697
O   Remnant Shop (fabric remnants; discount: 25–50%)

Jupiter
O   The Shoe Barn (shoes for the entire family; discount: 20–50%)

Lauderdale Lakes
O   Famous Name Shoes, Inc. (shoes for men and women; discount: 30%)

SA, G   **Miami**
O   Dorissa Children's World (girls' and boys' sportswear; discount: 40–60%)
R   Dressy I, 2124 N.E. 123rd St., (305) 891–1255
J   Encore Shop
R   Fashion II, 2122 S.W. 67th Ave., (305) 261–7892
DD   Loehmann's (women's clothing; discount: 20–70%)
R   Second Debut, 712 N.E. 128th St., (305) 891–7918
R   The Second Time Around, 4041 S.W. 96th Ave., (305) 223–1330

SA, G   **Orlando**
J   Bargain Box
R   Donna Lee's Shop, 645 Hoffner Ave., (305) 855–6555
R   My & Your Closet, 2905 Corrine Dr., (305) 894–5271

Palm Beach
J   Junior League Thrift Shop

Pompano Beach
DD   Loehmann's (women's clothing; discount: 20–70%)

SA, G   **St. Petersburg**
J   Junior League Thrift Shop
G   **Tallahassee**
J   Bargain Box
SA   **Tampa**

Tarpon Springs
DD   Loehmann's (women's clothing; discount: 20–70%)

G   **West Palm Beach**
R   Second Hand Rose of Park Avenue, Inc., 939 Park Ave., (305) 844–3140

(women's and children's clothing)

GEORGIA
G   **Albany**
SA, G **Atlanta**
O   Clothes Bin (sportswear; discount: 30–75%)
R   Encore, 2140 Henderson Mill Rd. NE, (404) 938–3555
O   Friedman's Shoes of Buckhead (men's and women's shoes; discount: 50%)
DD   Loehmann's (women's clothing; discount: 20–70%)
DD   Marshall's (men's, women's and children's clothes; discount: 20–70%)
J   Nearly New Shop
R   Play It Again, 273 Buckhead Ave. NE, (404) 261–2135
O   Southland Outlet Store (junior and misses' apparel)

Augusta
O   Just Kids (children's clothes; discount: 50%)

Bainbridge
O   Hi-Style Factory Outlet (ladies' clothing; discount: 10–75%)

Cobb
DD   Loehmann's (women's clothing; discount: 20–70%)

Cobb/Marietta
J   Bargain Shop
G   **Columbus**

DeKalb
DD   Loehmann's (women's clothing; discount: 20–70%)

East Point
O   Darsey Mfg. Co. (men's suits, sportscoats, slacks, shirts, ties, belts and socks; discount: 50%)
G   **Macon**
G   **Rome**

Sandy Springs
DD   Marshall's (men's, women's and children's clothes; discount: 20–70%)
G   **Savannah**

DD = Designer Discount; G = Goodwill; J = Junior League; O = Outlet; R = Resale; SA = Salvation Army.

Stone Mountain

DD   Marshall's (men's, women's and children's clothes; discount: 20–70%)

HAWAII

SA, G   **Honolulu**

IDAHO

Boise

R   Char-D's Bargain Boutique, 4111 Rose Hill, (208) 336-3531 (clothing for the entire family)

R   Kitty's, 13 E. Franklin Rd., Meridian, (208) 888-0061

R   Nearly Nu, 3117 W. State, (208) 343-0382

J   Second Time Around, 3113 Overland Rd., (208) 344-0760

Nampa

O   Ashley's—The Outlet Store (family apparel; discount: 50–60%)

ILLINOIS

Aurora

O   Arbetman Brothers (women's coats; discount: 50%)

O   Prevue Fashions (misses', women's and junior dresses; discount: 30–70%)

Berwyn

DD   Marshall's (men's, women's and children's clothes; discount: 20–70%)

SA   **Chicago**

O   Adams Factory Shoe Outlet (men's, women's and children's shoes; discount: 20–40%)

O   Children's Sample Apparel (children's clothing; discount: 30%)

R   Divine Idea Clothes, 2959 N. Clark, (312) 975-0909 (men's and women's vintage, new wave, 40's and 50's clothes)

O   Independent Clothing (men's and women's clothing; discount: 20–40%)

R   Lakeshore Resale Shop, 611 N. State, (312) 337–8987 (men's clothing)

DD   Loehmann's (women's clothing; discount: 20–70%)

R   Once More With Feeling, 1167 Wilmette, (312) 256-4554

R   Y-Not Resale Shop, 6116 N. Lincoln, (312) 281–6636

Collinsville

O   Factory Outlet Store (junior and misses' clothes; discount: 40–70%)

Countryside

DD   Marshall's (men's, women's and children's clothes; discount: 20–70%)

Downers Grove

DD   Loehmann's (women's clothing; discount: 20–70%)

Evanston

J   Thrift House

Highland Park

DD   Marshall's (men's, women's and children's clothes; discount: 20–70%)

Hoffman Estates

DD   Marshall's (men's, women's and children's clothes; discount: 20–70%)

Lombard

DD   Marshall's (men's, women's and children's clothes; discount: 20–70%)

Matteson

DD   Marshall's (men's, women's and children's clothes; discount: 20–70%)

Morton Grove

DD   Loehmann's (women's clothing; discount: 20–70%)

DD   Marshall's (men's, women's and children's clothes; discount: 20–70%)

Mt. Prospect

DD   Marshall's (men's, women's and children's clothes; discount: 20–70%)

Oaklawn

DD   Marshall's (men's, women's and children's clothes; discount: 20–70%)

DD = Designer Discount; G = Goodwill; J = Junior League; O = Outlet; R = Resale; SA = Salvation Army.

SA, G	**Peoria**
SA, G	**Rockford**
SA, G	**Springfield**
R	The Blue Parrot, 217½ S. 6th, (217) 525–1114
R	Jus-Lik-Nu-Shop, 2611 S. 1st, (217) 544–6552
SA	**Waukegan**

INDIANA

SA, G	**Evansville**
SA, G	**Fort Wayne**
J	Bargain Box
	Franklin
O	Carter Factory Outlet (infants' and children's clothing; discount: 30–60%)
SA, G	**Gary**
G	**Hammond**
SA, G	**Indianapolis**
R	The Almost New Shoppe, 8974 E. 10th, (317) 898–0485
O	Company Store (men's and women's clothing; discount: 60%)
R	Dorothy Kent's Nearly New Shop, 2258 N. Meridian, Suite B, (317) 924–4489
O	Les Kids Sample Shop (infants through teens; discount: 35%)
R	New to You Fashion Shop, 5216 N. College Ave., (317) 283–3683
J	Next to New Shop
O	Outlet (name brands; discount: 60%)
	Merrillville
O	Quality Discount Apparel (men's clothing; discount: 50%)
	Nashville
O	Shop and Save Store (family wear; discount: 50%)
G	**New Albany**
	Plymouth
O	Little Red School House (men's, women's and children's shoes; discount: 20–40%)

SA, G	**South Bend**
G	**Terre Haute**

IOWA

	Cedar Rapids
R	The Second Act, 122 Town & Country Shopping Ctr., (319) 363–2437
	Centerville
O	Ashley's—The Outlet Store (family apparel; discount: 40–60%)
	Chariton
O	Ashley's—The Outlet Store (family apparel; discount: 40–60%)
	Cherokee
O	Ashley's—The Outlet Store (family apparel; discount: 40–60%)
SA	**Davenport**
SA, G	**Des Moines**
J	Bargain Basket
R	Clothing Resell Shop, 2310 University, (515) 277–7392
R	Guys and Dolls Consignment Shop, 2215 W. Des Moines, (515) 255–7806
R	Village Peddler Ladies Consignment Shop, 2305 W. Des Moines, (515) 277–0330
	El Dorado
O	Ashley's—The Outlet Store (family apparel; discount: 40–60%)
	Fort Madison
O	Ashley's—The Outlet Store (family apparel; discount: 40–60%)
	Indianola
O	Lark Factory Outlet (name brands; discount: 50%)
G	**Iowa City**
	Le Mars
O	Ashley's—The Outlet Store (family apparel; discount: 40–60%)
	Marshalltown
O	Ashley's—The Outlet Store (family apparel; discount: 40–60%)

DD = Designer Discount; G = Goodwill; J = Junior League; O = Outlet; R = Resale; SA = Salvation Army.

Mt. Pleasant

O   Ashley's—The Outlet Store (family apparel; discount: 40–60%)

Newton

O   Ashley's—The Outlet Store (family apparel; discount: 40–60%)

O   Lark Factory Outlet (name brands; discount: 50%)

Osceola

O   Lark Factory Outlet (name brands; discount: 50%)

Oskaloosa

O   Ashley's—The Outlet Store (family apparel; discount: 40–60%)

Perry

O   Lark Factory Outlet (name brands; discount: 50%)

Sioux City

G
J   Discovery Shop

Washington

O   Ashley's—The Outlet Store (family apparel; discount: 40–60%)

G   **Waterloo**

KANSAS

Coffeyville

O   Ashley's—The Outlet Store (family apparel; discount: 40–60%)

Dodge City

O   Ashley's—The Outlet Store (family apparel; discount: 40–60%)

Edwardsville

O   Factory Outlet Store (men's clothing; discount: 30–50%)

Kansas City

R   Harry Kaufman Co., 1544 Iron, (816) 421-8244

J   Nearly New Shop

R   Pastimes, 4039 Broadway, (816) 753-9335

Liberal

O   Ashley's—The Outlet Store (family apparel; discount: 40–60%)

Overland Park

DD   Loehmann's (women's cloth-

ing; discount: 20–70%)

DD   Marshall's (men's, women's and children's clothes; discount: 20–70%)

Paola

O   Factory Outlet Store (men's clothing; discount: 30–50%)

Pittsburg

O   Ashley's—The Outlet Store (family apparel; discount: 40–60%)

O   Factory Outlet Store (men's clothing; discount: 30–50%)

G   **Wichita**
J   Junior League Thrift Shop

KENTUCKY

SA   **Bellevue**

Jefferson

O   Strasberg's (handbags, misses' and junior sportswear; discount: 25–50%)

SA   **Latonia**

Lexington

O   The Garment District (apparel for the family; discount: 20–75%)

SA, G **Louisville**

R   Act II Consignment Shop, 111 Wiltshire Ave., (502) 897-2806 (name-brand samples)

R   The Clothes Rack, 3762 Oakdale Ave., (502) 368-2807 (current styles for the entire family)

O   Goldy's Shoe Mart (brand-name dress shoes; discount: 20–40%)

R   Nearly New Clothing, 632 E. Market, (502) 584-4759

O   Williams Shoe Store (children's shoes; discount: 50%)

Shelbyville

O   Fashion Shop (buy-out from stores and manufacturers; discount: 30–50%)

LOUISIANA

Alexandria

J   New to You

DD = Designer Discount; G = Goodwill; J = Junior League; O = Outlet; R = Resale; SA = Salvation Army.

Baton Rouge
J   Nearly Nu
R   Second Glance Dress Shop,
    6636 Florida Blvd., (504)
    926-8250
Bossier City
O   Sondra's Factory Outlet
    (fabrics on bolts and rem-
    nants in boxes; discount:
    20-40%)
Lake Charles
O   Bevo's (name brands, junior
    and misses' sportswear and
    dresses; discount: 60%)
J   Nearly New Shop
SA, G **New Orleans**
R   Betsy's Bargain Basement,
    829 Derbigny, (504)
    361-5561
O   Clothing Showroom of La.,
    Inc. (men's clothing; dis-
    count: 40-65%)
J   Junior League Thrift Shop
G   **Shreveport**

MAINE

Augusta
O   Mill Fabrics Center (rem-
    nants and pound goods; dis-
    count: 30-40%)
SA **Bath**
SA **Biddeford**
Brewer
O   Emple Knitting Mills Factory
    Outlet (sweaters for the
    family; discount: 20-40%)
Dexter
O   Dexter Shoe Factory Outlet
    (men's, women's and chil-
    dren's shoes; discount:
    50%)
Ellsworth
O   Coastal Fashion Outlet
    (misses' and junior casual
    sportswear; discount: 60%)
SA, G **Portland**
J   Thrifty Yankee
SA **Raymond**
South Portland
DD Marshall's (men's, women's
    and children's clothes; dis-
    count: 20-70%)

MARYLAND

G   **Baltimore**
O   Batco Warehouse Shoe
    (shoes for the entire family;
    discount: 50%)
R   Carol's Thrift Shop, 6202
    Reisterstown Rd., (301)
    358-8296
R   Clothes Closet Unlimited,
    3996 Roland Ave., (301)
    243-9506
R   Just A Second Boutique,
    5708 Newbury St., (301)
    542-4450 (women's
    clothing)
O   Merry Go Round Warehouse
    Clothing Outlet (ladies' and
    men's wear; discount:
    40-60%)
R   National Fashion Exchange
    Inc., 5430 Lynx La., (301)
    997-4319 (ladies', men's,
    children's and maternity
    clothing)
O   Sam Oidick and Sons (men's
    clothing; discount: 75%)
J   Wise Penny
Cumberland
O   Allegheny Factory Outlet (in-
    fants' sleep, play and
    sportswear; discount: 50%)
G   **Frederick**
Greenbelt
DD Marshall's (men's, women's
    and children's clothes; dis-
    count: 20-70%)
G   **Hagerstown**
O   E. J. Fashions Inc. (women's
    sportswear and dresses;
    discount: 10-50%)
Rockville
DD Loehmann's (women's cloth-
    ing; discount: 20-70%)
SA **Suitland**
Towson
DD Loehmann's (women's cloth-
    ing; discount: 20-70%)

MASSACHUSETTS

Bedford
DD Marshall's (men's, women's
    and children's clothes; dis-
    count: 20-70%)

DD = Designer Discount; G = Goodwill; J = Junior League; O = Outlet; R = Resale;
SA = Salvation Army.

Berkshire
J   Junior League Thrift Shop
SA,G **Boston**
O   Adams Warehouse (men's fashion; discount: 50–85%)
J   Bargain Box
R   Encore Quality Consignment Shop, 68–A Billings Rd., (617) 328–1179
O   Filene's Dept. Store Basement (women's clothes—seconds and overstock; discount: 25–50%)
R   Pass It On, Kids, 23 Harvard, (617) 277–1320 (children's and maternity clothing)
R   Second Appearance, 801 Washington, (617) 527–7655 (men's and women's clothing)
SA **Brockton**
    Burlington
DD Loehmann's (women's clothing; discount: 20–70%)
SA **Cambridge**
    Canton
DD Marshall's (men's, women's and children's clothes; discount: 20–70%)
    Chelmsford
DD Marshall's (men's, women's and children's clothes; discount: 20–70%)
SA **Chelsea**
    Danvers
DD Marshall's (men's, women's and children's clothes; discount: 20–70%)
SA **Dorchester**
SA **Fall River**
SA **Fitchburg**
SA **Framingham**
DD Marshall's (men's, women's and children's clothes; discount: 20–70%)
O   Sportswear Store (brand-name clothing for the family; discount: 40–60%)
    Franklin
DD Marshall's (men's, women's

and children's clothes; discount: 20–70%)
    Hingham
DD Marshall's (men's, women's and children's clothes; discount: 20–70%)
SA **Holyoke**
J   Bargain Box
SA **Hyannis**
SA **Hyde Park**
    Leominster
DD Marshall's (men's, women's and children's clothes; discount: 20–70%)
SA,G **Lowell**
SA **Lynn**
O   Hoffman's (ladies', men's and children's shoes; discount: 40–60%)
    Marlboro
DD Marshall's (men's, women's and children's clothes; discount: 20–70%)
    Marshfield
DD Marshall's (men's, women's and children's clothes; discount: 20–70%)
    Medford
DD Marshall's (men's, women's and children's clothes; discount: 20–70%)
    Natick
DD Loehmann's (women's clothing; discount: 20–70%)
SA **New Bedford**
    Newton
DD Marshall's (men's, women's and children's clothes; discount: 20–70%)
SA,G **Pittsfield**
    Reading
DD Marshall's (men's, women's and children's clothes; discount: 20–70%)
SA **Southbridge**
    South Weymouth
DD Marshall's (men's, women's and children's clothes; discount: 20–70%)
SA,G **Springfield**

DD = Designer Discount; G = Goodwill; J = Junior League; O = Outlet; R = Resale; SA = Salvation Army.

J   Junior League Budget Box

DD   Marshall's (men's, women's and children's clothes; discount: 20–70%)

Swampscott

DD   Loehmann's (women's clothing; discount: 20–70%)

DD   Marshall's (men's, women's and children's clothes; discount: 20–70%)

Tewksbury

DD   Marshall's (men's, women's and children's clothes; discount: 20–70%)

Waltham

O   Hill Brothers (discontinued catalog styles; discount: 30–70%)

West Warren

O   Wrights Mill Store and American Home (remnants; discount: 50–70%)

Winchester

O   Topsy Turvy Inc. (famous brands in children's wear and accessories; discount: 40%)

SA   **Worcester**

J   Junior League Shop

MICHIGAN

G   **Adrian**

Ann Arbor

O   Claudin's Fashions (misses' and junior fashions; discount: 60%)

R   Kay's Klothes Kloset, 2370 E. Stadium Blvd., (313) 971–6211

R   The Tree, 419 Detroit, (313) 663–2008

G   **Battle Creek**

Bay City

O   Remnant Shoppe (remnants, quilted nylon and satin; discount: 50%)

Berkley

O   Lou D. Sales (men's clothing; discount: 30–40%)

Birmingham

J   The Bargain Box

SA, G   **Detroit**

R   Clothesport, 627 W. 9 Mile Rd., (313) 398–5019

O   "Good-Buy" Shop (children's, misses' and junior-miss clothes; discount: 50%)

R   Kidstuff, 2156 Plainfield NE, (313) 361–1060

R   Lee's Inc., 20339 Mack Grosse Pointe Woods, (313) 881–8082

R   Rags to Britches, 674 Baldwin, (313) 457–4630

O   Shoe Fair Stores (men's, women's, children's and infants' shoes; discount: 20–50%)

R   Twice Is Nice Consignment Boutique, 17 Squires St., (313) 866–9225

Farmington Hills

DD   Loehmann's (women's clothing; discount: 20–70%)

SA   **Flint**

SA, G   **Grand Rapids**

Ithaca

O   Okum Brothers Shoe Store (footwear for the entire family; discount: 25–60%)

G   **Jackson**

G   **Kalamazoo**

Lansing

J   Cedar Chest

O   Cut Label (men's and women's clothing; discount: 50–70%)

SA   **Pontiac**

G   **Port Huron**

Rochester

O   Clothes Press (men's, women's and children's clothing; discount: 25–60%)

O   Kid's Korner (brand-name clothing for children and infants thru size 14; discount: 50%)

Royal Oak

O   Clothing Warehouse (men's clothing; discount: 40–60%)

O   Salon Shoes Discount Outlet (name-brand women's shoes; discount: 20–50%)

DD = Designer Discount; G = Goodwill; J = Junior League; O = Outlet; R = Resale; SA = Salvation Army.

Saginaw
J   Junior League Wise Penney

MINNESOTA

Bloomington
DD   Loehmann's (women's cloth-
     ing; discount: 20–70%)

G   **Duluth**
SA   **Minneapolis**
R   The Clothes Horse, 1614 W.
     Lake St., (612) 822–6600
     (women's clothing)
J   The Clothes Line
O   D. B. Rosenblatt Retail Store
     (men's and women's cloth-
     ing; discount: 35–70%)
R   Little Sprouts, 6258 W. Lake
     St., (612) 929–6221 (chil-
     dren's clothing)
O   Munsingwear Remnant Room
     (fabrics; discount: 40–70%)
O   Nates Clothing Company
     (men's suits; discount:
     30–50%)
R   The Pink Closet, 4024 E.
     46th St., (612) 724–2468
     (men's, women's and chil-
     dren's clothing)
R   Rosie's Closet, 3539 W. 44th
     St., (612) 922–7363
     (women's clothing)
O   Sharpe Factory Store
     (women's and children's
     clothing; discount: 30–50%)
R   Upton Alley, 4303 Upton
     Ave. S, (612) 926–1446
     (children's through teens'
     and maternity clothing)

Robbinsdale
O   Children's Sample Shop
     (sample clothing for infants,
     boys, girls and teens; dis-
     count: 30–90%)

St. Cloud
O   Fingerhut Outlet (cloth-
     ing for the entire family;
     discount: 50%)

G   **St. Paul**
R   Klothes Klosett, 649 Snelling
     Ave. S, (612) 698–3484
     (men's and women's
     clothing)
J   Next to New

R   Tot's Trad'n Post, 832 White
     Bear Ave., (612) 738–9390
     (children's clothing)

Stillwater
O   Conn-Co Shoes (footwear for
     the entire family; discount:
     20–50%)

MISSISSIPPI

Bellefontaine
O   J. V. Wilson Leather Co.
     (ladies' western purses and
     billfolds; discount: 30%)

Brookhaven
O   Ashley's—The Outlet Store
     (family apparel; discount:
     50–60%)

G   **Gulfport**
G   **Jackson**
O   Ellis Men's Clothing (men's
     wear; discount: 40–50%)

Pass Christian
O   Melody Lane's Women's
     Apparel (women's wear;
     discount: 30–80%)

MISSOURI

Ballwin
DD   Marshall's (men's, women's
     and children's clothing; dis-
     count: 20–70%)

Branson
O   Clothes Factory Outlet (boys'
     and men's clothing; dis-
     count: 35–75%)

Cape Girardeau
O   Cape Outlet Shoes (famous-
     brand shoes for men and
     women; discount: 30–70%)

Florissant
DD   Marshall's (men's, women's
     and children's clothing; dis-
     count: 20–70%)

Hazelwood
O   Tops and Trousers (men's
     clothing; discount: 40–50%)

SA, G **Kansas City**
R   Harry Kaufman Co., 1544
     Iron, (816) 421–8244 (cloth-
     ing for the entire family)
J   Junior League Thrift Shop
O   Nor-Kay Factory (junior and

misses' clothes; discount:
30–60%)

R   Pastimes, 4039 Broadway,
(816) 753–9335

St. Joseph
J   Junior League Thrift Shop

SA, G **St. Louis**
O   Evelyn's Ladies and Chil-
dren's Fashion (children's
and women's clothes; dis-
count: 30–70%)
R   My Friends Wardrobe, 109
N. Kirkwood, (314)
821–8999
R   Second Time Around
Shoppe, 13145 New Halls
Ferry Rd., (314) 837–5117
R   Wear Else Inc., 8109 Big
Bend Blvd., (314) 961–1457

Springfield
J   The Plaid Door

Sullivan
O   Sullivan Factory Outlet
(men's and women's shoes;
discount: 20–50%)

Sunset Hills
DD   Marshall's (men's, women's
and children's clothing; discount: 20–70%)

MONTANA

Butte
R   The Repeat Boutique, 118 W.
Broadway, (406) 792–4994

G   **Great Falls**

NEBRASKA

Columbus
O   Ashley's—The Outlet Store
(family apparel; discount:
50–60%)

Falls City
O   Ashley's—The Outlet Store
(family apparel; discount:
50–60%)

G   **Grand Island**

Hastings
O   Ashley's—The Outlet Store
(family apparel; discount:
50–60%)

Holdrege
O   Ashley's—The Outlet Store

(family apparel; discount:
50–60%)

SA, G **Lincoln**
J   Junior League Thrift Shop
R   One More Time, 1325 South,
(308) 474–2064

Nebraska City
O   Ashley's—The Outlet Store
(family apparel; discount:
50–60%)
O   Pendleton Outlet (men's and
women's clothing; discount:
50%)

SA, G **Omaha**
J   Jumble Shop

NEVADA

G   **Las Vegas**
O   The Apparel Factory (sports-
wear; discount: 30–60%)
J   Repeat Boutique
R   Second Time Boutique, 2416
Ogden Ave., (702)
386–1763

NEW HAMPSHIRE

Bedford
DD   Marshall's (men's, women's
and children's clothing; discount: 20–70%)

Keene
O   Douglas Co. Factory Store
(children's clothes; dis-
count: 10–30%)

Littleton
O   Saranac Factory Store
(women's clothing; dis-
count: 40–65%)

SA, G **Manchester**
O   Bee Bee Shoe Store (shoes
for every member of the
family; discount: 20–40%)
O   Pandora Factory Store
(women's clothing; dis-
count: 40–65%)

Nashua
O   Kimbricks (brand-name
clothes for men, women
and children; discount:
50%)
DD   Marshall's (men's, women's
and children's clothing; discount: 20–70%)

---

*DD = Designer Discount; G = Goodwill; J = Junior League; O = Outlet; R = Resale;
SA = Salvation Army.*

Portsmouth
DD   Marshall's (men's, women's and children's clothing; discount: 20–70%)
O   Sweaterville U.S.A. (famous name-brand sweaters for the whole family; discount: 50%)

Salem
DD   Marshall's (men's, women's and children's clothing; discount: 20–70%)

NEW JERSEY

SA   **Atlantic City**
R   Act II Shop, 2 S. Montgomery Ave., (609) 347–2619

SA   **Bayonne**

Belmar
O   Bazaar No. 3—Factory Outlet (junior and misses' clothes; discount: 50%)

Bergen County
J   Second Hand Roses

Brick Town
O   Prints 'N' Plains Inc. (fabrics; discount: 40–60%)

Burlington
O   Burlington F. Whse. (famous-maker ladies', children's and men's wear; discount: 20–60%)

Camden
R   The Children's Exchange, 110 Ellis, (609) 428–8688
R   Merel's Resale Designer, Clothing and Accessories, 68 E. Main, (609) 234–4954

Cherry Hill
O   Doral Women's Fashion (junior and misses' clothing; discount: 20–40%)

SA   **Clifton**

SA   **Dover**

East Brunswick
DD   Loehmann's (women's clothing; discount: 20–70%)
DD   Marshall's (men's, women's and children's clothing; discount: 20–70%)

SA   **East Orange**

Edison
DD   Marshall's (men's, women's and children's clothing; discount: 20–70%)

SA   **Elizabeth/Plainfield**
J   Jumble Store

Elmer
O   Chatham Outlets (junior and misses' clothing; discount: 30–50%)

Florham Park
DD   Loehmann's (women's clothing; discount: 20–70%)

SA   **Hadden Heights**
G   **Harrison**
SA   **Hoboken**
SA   **Jersey City**
SA   **Montclair**

Moorestown
DD   Marshall's (men's, women's and children's clothing; discount: 20–70%)

Morristown
J   Nearly New Shop
SA   **Motclair**
SA   **Newark**
SA   **North Bergen**

Orange and Short Hills
J   Act II

Paramus
DD   Loehmann's (women's clothing; discount: 20–70%)
DD   Syms Clothing Inc. (men's, women's and children's clothes; discount: 30–60%)

SA   **Paterson**

Pennsauken
DD   Loehmann's (women's clothing; discount: 20–70%)
O   Shoe Town (shoes, boots, bedroom slippers; discount: 40%)

SA   **Perth Amboy**
SA   **Pompton Lakes**

Roselle
O   Regent Clothes (men's and boys' clothing; discount: 30%)

DD = Designer Discount; G = Goodwill; J = Junior League; O = Outlet; R = Resale; SA = Salvation Army.

SA **Salem**

Shewsbury
DD Marshall's (men's, women's and children's clothing; discount: 20–70%)

Summit
J Thrift and Consignment Shop

SA **Trenton**

Wayne
DD Marshall's (men's, women's and children's clothing; discount: 20–70%)

West Caldwell
DD Marshall's (men's, women's and children's clothing; discount: 20–70%)

Woodbridge
DD Syms Clothing Inc. (men's, women's and children's clothes; discount: 30–60%)

NEW MEXICO

G **Albuquerque**
R Bean Stalk, 3420 San Mateo NE, (505) 884–6688 (infants' and children's clothing)
O Factory Outlet Store (men's and women's clothing; discount: 33–50%)
O Famous Brand Factory Outlet (boys' and men's wear; discount: 50%)
R Jan's Ritzy Rags, 2823 San Mateo Blvd. NE, (505) 883–8755 (women's clothing)
R Second Chance Consignment Shop, 3004-D Central Ave. SE, (505) 266–4266

G **Las Cruces**

NEW YORK

SA **Albany**
J Next to New Shop

SA **Astoria**

SA **Auburn**

SA **Babylon**

SA **Batavia**

Bayshore
DD Loehmann's (women's clothing; discount: 20–70%)

Belle Harbor
O Earl's (women's clothing; discount: 30–65%)

SA **Binghamton**

SA **Bronx**
DD Loehmann's (women's clothing; discount: 20–70%)

Bronxville
J Penny Pincher Shop

SA **Brooklyn**
DD Loehmann's (women's clothing; discount: 20–70%)
R Thrifty Threads for Kids, 2082 E. 13th St., (212) 336–8037

SA,G **Buffalo**
R Bargain Rack, 555 Englewood Ave., (716) 836–9109 (clothing for the entire family)
R Eleanor's Trading Post, 2267 Delaware Ave., (716) 874–5888
R The Clothes Horse, 3527 Orchard Park Rd., (716) 662–1136
DD Syms Clothing Inc. (men's, women's and children's clothing; discount: 30–60%)
R Thru the Grape Vine, 706 Terce Blvd., (716) 681-1943

Carle Place
DD Marshall's (men's, women's and children's clothing; discount: 20–70%)

SA **Central Islip**

SA **Chittenango**

SA **Colonie**

SA **Cortland**

East Islip
DD Marshall's (men's, women's and children's clothing; discount: 20–70%)

SA **Elmira**

SA **Elmont**

SA **Endicott**

SA **Fredonia**

SA **Freeport**

SA **Fulton**

SA **Geneva**

DD = Designer Discount; G = Goodwill; J = Junior League; O = Outlet; R = Resale; SA = Salvation Army.

SA	**Glens Falls**
SA	**Glenville**
SA	**Gloversville**
SA	**Hempstead**
	Hewlett
DD	Loehmann's (women's clothing; discount: 20–70%)
SA	**Huntington**
DD	Loehmann's (women's clothing; discount: 20–70%)
DD	Marshall's (men's, women's and children's clothing; discount: 20–70%)
SA	**Ilion**
SA	**Irondequiot**
SA	**Ithaca**
	Jamaica
O	Shoe Giant Outlet (name-brand shoes for the entire family; discount: 60%)
SA	**Jamestown**
SA	**Kenmore**
SA	**Kingston**
SA	**Latham**
SA	**Levittown**
	Long Island
DD	Syms Clothing Inc. (men's, women's and children's clothing; discount: 30–60%)
	Manhattan
O	Active Clothing (men's wear; discount: 30–70%)
O	Barall, Louis and Son (men's clothing; discount: 20–50%)
O	Bargain Basement (ladies' handbags and accessories; discount: 30–50%)
DD	The Best Things Outlet (women's clothing; discount: 30–50%)
O	De Silva (men's clothing; discount: 35–70%)
R	Encore Resale Dress Shop, 1132 Madison Ave., (212) 874-2850
R	Exchange Unlimited, 563 2nd Ave., (212) 889-3229 (clothing for the entire family)
O	Fashion Discount (children's clothing; discount: 20–50%)

O	Finecraft Knitwear (women's clothing; discount: 30–65%)
O	Jim Salzman Shoes (men's shoes; discount: 30–60%)
R	Michael's Resale Shop, 78th and Madison Ave., (212) 737-7273
R	Second Story, Ltd., 1400 3rd Ave., (212) 535-2417 (women's clothing)
R	Second Act, Resale Children's Apparel, 1046 Madison Ave., (212) 988-2440
DD	Syms Clothing Inc. (men's, women's and children's clothing; discount: 30–60%)
	Mt. Kisco
DD	Loehmann's (women's clothing; discount: 20–70%)
SA	**Mount Vernon**
	Nanuet
DD	Marshall's (men's, women's and children's clothing; discount: 20–70%)
SA	**Newburgh**
	New Hyde Park
DD	Loehmann's (women's clothing; discount: 20–70%)
SA	**New Paltz**
SA	**New Rochelle**
SA, G	**New York City**
SA	**Niagara Falls**
	Northern Westchester
J	The Thrift Shop
	North Shore
J	Junior League Thrift Shop
SA	**North Syracuse**
SA	**Oneida**
SA	**Oneonta**
SA	**Oswego**
SA	**Patchogue**
SA	**Peekskill**
	Pelham
J	The Magic Closet
SA	**Perth Amboy**
SA	**Port Chester**
SA	**Poughkeepsie**
J	Bargain Box

DD Marshall's (men's, women's and children's clothing; discount: 20-70%)

Queens
DD Loehmann's (women's clothing; discount: 20-70%)
SA **Riverhead**
SA **Rochester**
SA **Rome**
SA **Salamanca**
SA **Spring Valley**
SA **Staten Island**
Stony Brook
DD Marshall's (men's, women's and children's clothing; discount: 20-70%)
SA **Syracuse**
SA **Utica**
O The Children's Outlet (infants', toddlers' and children's clothing; discount: 25-50%)
SA **Watertown**
Westchester
DD Syms Clothing Inc. (men's, women's and children's clothing; discount: 30-60%)
Westchester-On-Hudson
J The Nearly New Shop
Westchester-On-Sound
J The Golden Shoe String
SA **Westfield**
White Plains
DD Loehmann's (women's clothing; discount: 20-70%)
SA **Woodside**
SA **Yonkers**

NORTH CAROLINA
Asheboro
O Stedman Corp. Outlet Store (boys' and men's sportswear; discount: 30-65%)
O Walker Shoe Store (men's shoes; discount: 30-50%)
Asheville
J Next to New Shop
Burlington
O Kiddie Barn (infants' thru children's wear; discount:

20-50%)
O The Remnant Shop (fabrics; discount: 25-40%)
SA, G **Charlotte**
J Junior League Wearhouse
R Statesville Road Variety Store, 5407 Statesville Rd., (704) 596-0529
O Woonsocket Spinning Co. (men's and ladies' clothing; discount: 30-60%)
G **Durham**
Gaston County
J The Bargain Box
Gastonia
O SC's Factory Outlet (junior and ladies' name-brand clothing; discount: 50-75%)
G **Greensboro**
J The Bargain Box
High Point
J Junior League Bargain Boutique
Raleigh
J Bargain Box
G **Winston-Salem**

NORTH DAKOTA
Bismarck
R The Store, 931 S. 9th, (701) 258-2446
SA **Fargo**

OHIO
SA, G **Akron**
SA **Alliance**
O Bressan Shoe Factory Outlet (ladies' shoes; discount: 30-50%)
SA, G **Ashtabula**
SA **Barberton**
Bucyrus
O Vasil's Mfg. and Fabric (women's clothing; discount: 50-75%)
SA, G **Canton**
G **Chillicothe**
SA, G **Cincinnati**
DD Loehmann's (women's clothing; discount: 20-70%)

DD = Designer Discount; G = Goodwill; J = Junior League; O = Outlet; R = Resale; SA = Salvation Army.

O	Outlet Town Shoes (women's shoes; discount: 40–50%)
R	A Patchwork Orange, 2617 Vine, (513) 751–6583
R	Remains to Be Seen, 323 Ludlow Ave., (513) 281–7397
R	Scentiments, 2614 Vine, (513) 281–1667
O	Seymour Factory Outlet (women's clothing; discount: 50–75%)
O	White Oak Factory Outlet (women's clothing; discount: 50–75%)
SA, G	**Cleveland**
R	Alice's Clothing Exchange, 10200 Cedar, (216) 791–9170
R	The Apple Core, 25903 Detroit, (216) 835–4747
R	Lakewood Clothing & Resale Shop, 15725 Madison, (216) 228–5954
SA, G	**Columbus**
SA, G	**Dayton**
SA	**East Liverpool**
SA	**Elyria**
SA	**Findlay**
SA	**Hamilton**
G	**Lima**
SA	**Lockland**
SA, G	**Lorain**
G	**Marion**
SA	**Miamisburg**
SA	**Middletown**
G	**Newark**
SA	**Perrysburg**
G	**Portsmouth**
G	**Sandusky**
SA	**Sharon**
SA	**Springfield**
SA	**Stow**
SA, G	**Toledo**
SA	**Warren**
G	**Wooster**
SA	**Xenia**
SA, G	**Youngstown**

G	**Zanesville**

OKLAHOMA

Del City

O	Wall's Bargain Center (clothing and shoes for the entire family; discount: 30–75%)
G	**Lawton**
O	Outhose Factory Outlet (jeans; discount: 10–40%)
G	**Muskogee**
SA, G	**Oklahoma City**
R	The Bottom Drawer, 7620 N. Western, (405) 848–6111
O	Con-Stan Industries Inc., Warehouse and Retail Store (women's clothing; discount: 75%)
R	The Re-Finery, 3739 N.W. 50th, (405) 947–5442 (reusable women's clothing)
J	Remarkable Shop
SA, G	**Tulsa**

OREGON

G	**Eugene**
J	Thrift & Gift Shop
G	**Medford**
SA, G	**Portland**
R	Act Two, 1139 S.W. Morrison, (503) 227–7969 (women's clothing)
J	The Bargain Tree
R	Duds & Do Dads Boutique, 4404 S.E. 104th, (503) 761–3457
R	The Resale Rack, 122nd & S.E. Market (503) 253–9206
O	Sample Boutique (salesmen's samples; discount: 50%)
R	The Shady Lady, 823 N.W. 23rd, (503) 248–0518

PENNSYLVANIA

SA	**Allequippa**
SA	**Altoona**
O	Warnaco Outlet Store (clothing for the entire family; discount: 50%)
SA	**Beaver Falls**
	Bedford

DD = Designer Discount; G = Goodwill; J = Junior League; O = Outlet; R = Resale; SA = Salvation Army.

O	Cancellation Shoe Store (shoes for the family; discount: 25–50%)
SA	**Berwick**
SA	**Bloomsburg**
SA	**Braddock**
SA	**Brookline**
SA	**Carbondale**
SA	**Chester**
	Drexel Hill
DD	Loehmann's (women's clothing; discount: 20–70%)
G	**DuBois**
SA	**Easton**
SA	**Edwardsville**
SA	**Erie**
SA	**Eynon**
	Feasterville
O	Santerian's Factory to You Clothing (clothing for the entire family; discount: 30%)
SA	**Grove City**
G	**Harrisburg**
SA	**Hazelton**
SA	**Homestead**
G	**Johnstown**
	King of Prussia
DD	Marshall's (men's, women's and children's clothing; discount: 20–70%)
SA, G	**Lancaster**
J	Thrift Corner
	Langhorne
DD	Marshall's (men's, women's and children's clothing; discount: 20–70%)
SA	**Lansdale**
	Lebanon
O	Milsan Mills Outlet (men's, ladies' and boys' shirts, slacks, jeans and sportswear; discount: 50%)
SA	**Levittown**
	Lititz
O	B & V Outlet (men's, women's and children's clothing; discount: 50%)

SA	**Lyndora**
SA	**Marcus Hook**
	Marple/Springfield
DD	Marshall's (men's, women's and children's clothing; discount: 20–70%)
SA	**McKeesport**
SA	**McKees Rocks**
SA	**Meadville**
SA	**New Castle**
SA	**Norristown**
	North Wales
DD	Loehmann's (women's clothing; discount: 20–70%)
	Northeast Philadelphia
DD	Marshall's (men's, women's and children's clothing; discount: 20–70%)
SA, G	**Philadelphia**
R	The Extra Hanger, 30 Maplewood Ave., (215) 844–3906 (women's clothing)
J	Junior League Thrift Shop
SA, G	**Pittsburgh**
R	The Clothes Horse, 306 Beverly Rd., (412) 341–6400
J	The Junior League Shop
R	Second Best, 1325 Fifth Ave., (412) 391–1406
G	**Reading**
SA, G	**Scranton**
SA	**Stroudsburg**
SA	**Union City**
SA	**Wesleyville**
	West Reading
O	Mother Goose Children's Shoe Outlet (children's shoes; discount: 25–50%)
	Williamsport
J	Exchange Mart
	Willow Grove
DD	Marshall's (men's, women's and children's clothing; discount: 20–70%)
SA	**Wyoming**
	York
J	Junior League Thrift Shop

DD = Designer Discount; G = Goodwill; J = Junior League; O = Outlet; R = Resale; SA = Salvation Army.

RHODE ISLAND
Cranston
DD Marshall's (men's, women's and children's clothing; discount: 20–70%)
SA **East Greenwich**
SA **Pawtucket**
SA **Providence**
SA **Warwick**
O Hit or Miss (women's brand-name clothing; discount: 35–50%)
SA **West Warwick**

SOUTH CAROLINA
G **Charleston**
DD Loehmann's (women's clothing; discount: 20–70%)
Columbia
J Second Look
O Uncle Sam's Clothing Store (clothing for the whole family; discount: 20–50%)
G **Greenville**
O Cancellation Shoe Mart (ladies' shoes; discount: 50–60%)
J The Nearly New Shop
Salley
O Salley Factory Outlet (junior and women's clothing; discount: 50–70%)

SOUTH DAKOTA
Aberdeen
R Roncalli Nearly New Shop, 301 S.E. R.R. Ave., (605) 225-7121

TENNESSEE
Athens
O Athens Outlet Store (clothing for the family; discount: 20–50%)
Bristol
J Bargain Box
G **Chattanooga**
J Bargain Mart
O Topps Men's Wear Factory Outlet (men's clothing; discount: 40–50%)
Greenville

O Diamond G. Outlet Store (family clothing; discount: 40–70%)
Knoxville
J The Bargain Box
SA, G **Memphis**
J Junior League Thrift Shop
R Reminiscence, 28 Idlewild S., (901) 272-2820
SA, G **Nashville**
R Bargain Boutique, 4004 Hillsboro Rd., (615) 297-7900
R Something Old Something New Consignment Shoppe, 4002–A Granny White Pke., (615) 298-3134
Paris
O Campbell's Factory Outlet (jeans for the whole family; discount: 50%)
Pigeon Forge
O Village Peddler (ladies' and men's shoes; discount: 20–70%)

TEXAS
Almeda
DD Marshall's (men's, women's and children's clothing; discount: 20–70%)
G **Amarillo**
G **Austin**
R Act II Resale Shop, 3339 Hancock, (512) 451-0076 (children's, teens' and women's clothing)
R The Bazaar, 2404 Guadalupe, (512) 478-3536
J Junior League Thrift Shop
DD Loehmann's (women's clothing; discount: 20–70%)
R M'Lord's & M'Ladies' Closet, 5732 Burnet Rd., (512) 453-3263
R Second Time Around, 3704 Crawford, (512) 451-6845 (children's and women's clothing)
G **Beaumont**
G **Corpus Christi**
SA, G **Dallas**
O Barshops Factory Outlet

DD = Designer Discount; G = Goodwill; J = Junior League; O = Outlet; R = Resale; SA = Salvation Army.

Shoes (shoes for the entire family; discount: 35–75%)

R   Baubles & Beads Resale Boutique, 380 Promenade, (214) 690–4692

O   Children's Sample Mart (infants', children's, teens' and junior petites' clothes; discount: 25–50%)

R   Clotheshorse Anonymous Inc., 1413 Preston Forest Sq., (214) 233–6082

DD   Loehmann's (women's clothing; discount: 20–70%)

DD   Marshall's (men's, women's and children's clothing; discount: 20–70%)

R   My Sister's Closet, 2522 Oak Lawn, (214) 521–1675

R   Re-Threads for Men, 1450 Preston Forest Sq., (214) 233–1684

G   **El Paso**

SA, G   **Fort Worth**

O   Bogart Industries Man. Warehouse (women's clothing; discount: 50–75%)

R   The Consignment Store, 712 Dorothy Lane, (817) 732–5701

J   Double Exposure

R   Kid's Round-Up, 2304 W. Park Row Dr., (817) 460–9487 (sizes 0–14)

R   Reruns Resale Store, 5107 Pershing (817) 731–4355

R   Wardrobe Anonymous, 3017 Waits, (817) 924–1441

Hedwig Village

DD   Marshall's (men's, women's and children's clothing; discount: 20–70%)

SA, G   **Houston**

R   Between Us, 3612 S. Shepherd, (713) 527–9989

R   Biz & Beau's Resale Shop, 6369 Westheimer, (713) 781–1401

DD   Loehmann's (women's clothing; discount: 20–70%)

DD   Marshall's (men's, women's and children's clothing; discount: 20–70%)

R   Prior To, 5615 Morningside, (713) 524–8359

Lott

O   The Fair (men's, women's and children's clothes; discount: 30–50%)

G   **Lubbock**

Midland

J   Next to New Shop

Odessa

J   Junior League Thrift Shop

San Angelo

J   Junior League Thrift Shop

SA, G   **San Antonio**

R   Barbara's Next to New Shoppe, 112 N.W. Center Mall, (512) 732–1401; 5310–A Jackwood, (512) 681–4772 (clothing for the entire family)

DD   Loehmann's (women's clothing; discount: 20–70%)

O   San Antonio Outlet Store (men's clothing; discount: 20–70%)

O   Too Good to be Threw, 1319 N.E. Loop 410, (512) 828–4799

Sharpstown

DD   Marshall's (men's, women's and children's clothing; discount: 20–70%)

G   **Sherman**

G   **Tyler**

J   Bargain Box

G   **Waco**

J   Penny Pincher

UTAH

Provo

O   Joline Co. Inc. (girls' clothing; discount: 50%)

Salt Lake City

O   Brandalls (men's and women's clothing; discount: 50%)

R   Encore Sales, 1826 S. 900 St. E, (801) 466–2791

J   Junior League Thrift Shop

O   Shoe Fair (shoes for the whole family; discount: 50%)

DD = Designer Discount; G = Goodwill; J = Junior League; O = Outlet; R = Resale; SA = Salvation Army.

VERMONT

SA **Bennington**
SA **Burlington**
O Ginny's Factory Store (misses' and teens' clothing; discount: 40%)
R Pam's Place, 77 Main St., (802) 863–1461

Charlestown
O Charlestown Mill Store (sweaters for the entire family; discount: 30–75%)

Essex Junction
R The Exchange, 167 Pearl, (802) 878–3848

St. Johnsbury
O Hovey's Thrift Store (men's, women's and children's clothing; discount: 20–60%)

VIRGINIA

Alexandria
DD Marshall's (men's, women's and children's clothing; discount: 20–70%)
G **Danville**

Falls Church
DD Loehmann's (women's clothing; discount: 20–70%)
G **Gate City**

Independence
O Imperial Reading Corp. (men's and women's clothing; discount: 25–50%)
G **Norfolk**
O Lottie's Brand Name Discount Shoes (ladies' shoes; discount: 50%)
R Swap Shop, 3018 Victory Blvd., (804) 487–9493

Petersburg
O Shoe Shack (family shoes; discount: 30–75%)

SA, G **Richmond**
J The Clothes Rack
O Imp. Peddlar Ltd. (family clothing; discount: 25–40%)
G **Roanoke**

WASHINGTON

G **Aberdeen**

G **Pasco**
SA **Seattle**
R The Clothes Closet, 4137 California SW, (206) 938–2110 (clothing for the entire family)
DD Loehmann's (women's clothing; discount: 20–70%)
O Sample Boutique (sizes 5–12; discount: 30–50%)
J The Wise Penny
G **Spokane**
R The Back Room Boutique, 2001 W. Pacific, (509) 624–4701
R The Reclothery, 702 S. Washington, (509) 624–9741
SA, G **Tacoma**
J Second Closet
G **Walla Walla**

WEST VIRGINIA

G **Charleston**
G **Huntington**
Moundsville
O Mountaineer Leathers Inc. Outlet Store (men's and women's clothing; discount: 10–30%)

Parkersburg
J Junior League Shop
Richland
R Cheryl's Family Closet, 248 Williams Blvd., (304) 943–3344

Spencer
O Ashley's—The Outlet Store (family clothing; discount: 40–60%)

WISCONSIN

Green Bay
O The Remnant Shop (fabrics; discount: 25–60%)
G **Madison**
R Cheap Frills, 1835 Parmenter, (608) 831–3515
R Clothes Crossing, 3840 Atwood Ave., (608) 222–4142 (women's and children's clothing)
G **Milwaukee**

DD = Designer Discount; G = Goodwill; J = Junior League; O = Outlet; R = Resale; SA = Salvation Army.

R	Act II Consignment-Resale Shoppe, 4314 N. Oakland Ave., (414) 332–4140
O	Clothes Rack (name-brand women's clothing; discount: 50%)
R	East Town Women's Resale Shop, 104 E. Mason, (414) 276–3184
R	Elm Grove Resale & Sample Shoppe, 13300 Watertown Pk. Rd., (414) 786–5150 (clothing for the entire family)
DD	Loehmann's (women's clothing; discount: 20–70%)
R	Mason Resale, Ltd., 424 E. Wells, (414) 271–3015 (men's clothing)
J	Penny Wise Shop

Neenah

O	Jersild Store (men's and ladies' sweaters; discount: 40%)

Racine

G	**Racine**
J	The Attic

West Allis

O	Shoe Factory Outlet Store (women's and men's shoes, boots; discount: 60%)

WYOMING

SA	**Casper**
G	**Cheyenne**
O	Factory Wear House Outlet (family pants and shirts; discount: 30–60%)

CANADA

ALBERTA

SA	**Calgary**
J	Next to New Shop
SA, G	**Edmonton**

BRITISH COLUMBIA

SA	**Vancouver**
R	Boutique Exchange, 2461 Marine, W. Vancouver, (604) 922–6414
J	Junior League Thrift Shop
G	**Victoria**

MANITOBA

SA	**Winnipeg**
J	Junior League Thrift Shop
R	Second Helpings, 259 Lilac, (204) 453–3412 (children's clothing)

NEW BRUNSWICK

SA	**Saint John**

NEWFOUNDLAND

SA	**St. John's**

NOVA SCOTIA

SA	**Halifax**
J	Bargain Box

ONTARIO

SA	**Brantford**
SA, G	**Hamilton**
SA	**Kitchener**
SA, G	**London**
SA	**Ottawa**
SA	**St. Catharines**
G	**Sarnia**
SA	**Sudbury**
SA	**Thunder Bay**
SA, G	**Toronto**
R	Fashion Mine, 80 Scollard, (204) 923–3332
R	Frankel Clothing Exchange, 123 Church, (204) 366–4221
R	The Looking Glass, 394 E. Glinton W, (204) 487–1264
J	Opportunity Shop
SA, G	**Windsor**

QUEBEC

SA	**Montreal**
R	Boutique Fantasque De Marie Claire, 2155 de la Montagne, (514) 288–3655
J	La Ligue
R	Turnabout Shop, 386 Victoria, (514) 488–8262
SA	**Quebec City**

SASKATCHEWAN

SA	**Regina**
SA	**Saskatoon**

DD = Designer Discount; G = Goodwill; J = Junior League; O = Outlet; R = Resale; SA = Salvation Army.

Index

Free Stuff!

Free Stuff For Parents

Over 250 of the best free and up-to-a-dollar booklets and samples parents can get by mail: • *sample teether, baby spoon, safety latch and drinking cup* • *booklets on pregnancy, childbirth, child care, nutrition, health, safety, first aid, reading, day care* • *sample copies of parenting newsletters and magazines and mail order catalogs.* **Only $3.75 ppd.**

Free Stuff For Kids

Over 250 of the best free and up-to-a-dollar things kids can get by mail: • *badges & buttons* • *games, kits & puzzles* • *coins, bills & stamps* • *bumper stickers & decals* • *coloring & comic books* • *posters & maps* • *seeds & rocks.* FREE STUFF FOR KIDS is America's #1 best-selling book for children! **Only $3.75 ppd.**

Free Stuff For Cooks

Over 250 of the best free and up-to-a-dollar booklets and samples cooks can get by mail: • *cookbooks with more than 3,700 recipes for cooking with almonds, fish, wine, eggs, in microwave ovens, clay pots and more* • *money-saving shopping guides and nutrition information* • *sample popcorn ball maker, herb seeds, spices* • *sample food and couponing newsletters.* **Only $3.75 ppd.**

Free Stuff For Home & Garden

Over 350 of the best free and up-to-a-dollar booklets, catalogs and products the home handyman and gardener can get by mail: • *free plans for a new home or addition* • *22 ways to save energy heating and cooling a home* • *furniture-by-mail* • *sample seeds and plants* • *tips on landscaping and vegetable gardening* • *weatherproofing, insulating, and painting guides.* **Only $3.75 ppd.**

Free Stuff For Travelers

Over 1000 free and up-to-a-dollar things travelers can get by mail: • *camping information* • *colorful travel posters* • *festivals and free attractions* • *canoe trips and cruises* • *hotel and motel directories* • *state and national park information* • *beaches and resorts* • *skiing and sailing vacations* • *travel and safety tips* • *maps and guidebooks for thousands of destinations!* **Only $3.75 ppd.**

Meadowbrook's Tips

Family Doctor's Health Tips
by Keith Sehnert, M.D.

Finally, a complete health guide you can really use to take care of yourself! The art of staying in top-notch condition and stopping an illness before it stops you. Dr. Keith Sehnert tells how to adopt a healthier lifestyle, when to call a doctor and how to get the most for your health-care dollar. • *self-diagnosis and self-care* • *what to do before you call the doctor* • *fitness, nutrition and mental wellness programs* • *drug side effects* • *recognizing stress and removing it from your life.* **$5.75 ppd.**

Successful Dieting Tips
Compiled by Bruce Lansky

The reason most diets don't work is that dieter's can't stick to them. SUCCESSFUL DIETING TIPS contains over 1,000 proven ideas to help dieters start and stick to any diet, such as how to: • *select the diet that's best for you* • *overcome toughest diet temptations of favorite foods, holidays, and eating out* • *avoid binges and bounce back when you can't resist* • *maintain an ideal weight.* **Only $5.75 ppd.**

Best Practical Parenting Tips
by Vicki Lansky

Over 1,000 parent-tested ideas for baby and child care that you won't find in Dr. Spock's books. Vicki's newest bestseller is the most helpful collection of new, down-to-earth ideas from new parents ever published. Practical ideas for saving time, trouble and money on such topics as: • *new baby care* • *car travel* • *toilet training* • *dressing kids for less* • *discipline* • *self-esteem.* **Only $5.75 ppd.**

The Best European Travel Tips
by John Whitman

Here's what the other travel guides don't tell about Europe. Whitman's indispensable, easy-to-read tips tell how to avoid tourist traps, rip offs and snafus . . . and how to: • *avoid getting ripped-off on currency exchanges* • *get low-cost airfares, tours, hotel rates* • *get your travel documents quickly* • *get through customs quickly* • *how to beat no-vacancy at a hotel* • *how to keep your fanny from being pinched in Italy.* **Only $5.75 ppd.**

Order Form

BOOKS (Prices include postage and handling.)

_____ BEST EUROPEAN TRAVEL TIPS . . . . $5.75 ppd.
_____ BEST FREE ATTRACTIONS (EAST) . . . . $4.75 ppd.
_____ BEST FREE ATTRACTIONS (MIDWEST) . . . . $4.75 ppd.
_____ BEST FREE ATTRACTIONS (SOUTH) . . . . $4.75 ppd.
_____ BEST FREE ATTRACTIONS (WEST) . . . . $4.75 ppd.
_____ SUCCESSFUL DIETING TIPS . . . . $5.75 ppd.
_____ FAMILY DOCTOR'S HEALTH TIPS . . . . $5.75 ppd.
_____ FREE STUFF FOR COOKS . . . . $3.75 ppd.
_____ FREE STUFF FOR HOME & GARDEN . . . . $3.75 ppd.
_____ FREE STUFF FOR KIDS . . . . $3.75 ppd.
_____ FREE STUFF FOR PARENTS . . . . $3.75 ppd.
_____ FREE STUFF FOR TRAVELERS . . . . $3.75 ppd.
_____ BEST PRACTICAL PARENTING TIPS . . . . $5.75 ppd.

Name: _____

Address: _____

_____ Zip _____

If ordering more than 6 books, please write to us for quantity discount rates.

$ Total enclosed _____

Make checks payable to:
Meadowbrook Press, Dept. **DBFL-DM**
I bought my book at □ bookstore □ other retail store □ my bookclub